Untwisting

Scripture

TO FIND FREEDOM AND JOY
IN JESUS CHRIST

BOOK 4
WOLVES, HYPOCRISY, SIN LEVELING,
& RIGHTEOUSNESS

Rebecca Davis

New Morning Press

Copyright © 2022 Rebecca Davis.

All rights reserved. Except for brief excerpts, no part of this publication may be reproduced, distributed or transmitted in any form or by any means, including photocopying, recording, or other electronic or mechanical methods, without the prior written permission of the publisher, except in the case of brief quotations embodied in critical reviews and certain other noncommercial uses permitted by copyright law.

For permission requests and quantity discounts, write to the author, Rebecca Davis, via the website https://heresthejoy.com.

All Scriptures, unless otherwise noted, are from the Holy Bible, English Standard Version® (ESV®), copyright © 2001 by Crossway, a publishing ministry of Good News Publishers. Used by permission. All rights reserved.

Scriptures marked KJV are from The Holy Bible, King James Version.

Scriptures marked NIV are from The Holy Bible, New International Version®, copyright © 1973, 1978, 1984, 2011 by Biblica, Inc.™ Used by permission. All rights reserved worldwide.

Scriptures marked AMPC are from the Amplified® Bible Classic Edition, copyright © 1995 by The Lockman Foundation. Used by permission.

Scriptures marked NKJV are from the New King James Version. Copyright © 1982 by Thomas Nelson, Inc. All rights reserved. Used by permission.

Scriptures marked NET are from the New English Translation Bible® copyright ©1996-2016 by Biblical Studies Press, L.L.C. All rights reserved. Used by permission.

Scriptures marked JUB are from the Jubilee Bible 2000, Copyright © 2013, 2020, translated and edited by Russell M. Stendal. Used by permission.

Cover photo by Stephanie Council

Cover design by Tim Davis

Untwisting Scriptures to find freedom and joy in Jesus Christ: Book 4 wolves, hypocrisy, sin leveling, & righteousness / Rebecca Davis. —first edition.

ISBN 9798986548906

*Dedicated to the wonderful survivors
of cults and other spiritually abusive churches
who still long to know the true Jesus.
You are my heroes.*

Books in the *Untwisting Scriptures* series

Untwisting Scriptures
that were used to tie you up, gag you,
and tangle your mind

Book 1: Rights, Bitterness, and Taking Up Offenses
Book 2: Patriarchy and Authority
Book 3: Your Words, Your Emotions

Untwisting Scriptures
to Find Freedom and Joy in Jesus Christ

Book 4: Wolves, Hypocrisy, Sin Leveling, and Righteousness

Contents

First Thoughts: About Righteousness and Wickedness..7

PART 1: God's Children Are Not Vile and Disgusting But Have Full Access to Joyful Righteousness

1. Does God Need to "Look Through the Filter of Jesus" to See His Children? 11
2. Are You the Prodigal Son or the Older Brother?.................................... 17
3. Nothing Like the Sheep Sermon to Make You Feel Stupid, Disgusting, and Useless 23

PART 2: We Can Recognize and Reject Sin Leveling

4. What is "Sin Leveling" and What's Wrong With It?............................. 33
5. Pronoun Trouble in Romans 2 That Can Keep the Oppressed in a Place of Bondage.. 45
6. Why "I'm the Worst Sinner I Know" Is Unbiblical 53
7. How Teaching Christians to Embrace "I'm the Worst Sinner I Know" Harms the Body of Christ 67
8. To Those Who Say All Christians Are Hypocrites................................ 79
9. About That "Log in Your Own Eye"... 89

PART 3: We Can Be Wise About Wickedness, Wolves, and Hypocrisy

10. Making Sense of the Church's Epidemic of Abuse 99
11. On the Proliferation of Wolves in the Churches................................. 107
12. Don't "Err on the Side of Grace" 119
13. Jesus vs. the Vipers... 131

PART 4: We Can Flourish in Our Christian Lives

14. Why "Metanoia" is So Much Greater Than "Repentance"................ 141
15. Free from Sin.. 155
16. "Look to the Cross More": A Response to the "Gospel-Centered" Movement 167

Scripture Index.. 177
About the Author 180

FIRST THOUGHTS

About Righteousness and Wickedness

That's what this book is all about. What is righteousness? What is wickedness? And why do Christians need to understand these concepts?

This understanding is one of the most basic aspects of living in this world, and especially living as a Christian.

My first desire for this book is to help you, the one who seeks after God, who truly wants to know Him, to gain more clarity on what your life is really like within the righteousness of Jesus Christ.

My other desire is for you to gain more clarity in being able to distinguish the wolves from the sheep, the hypocrites from those with integrity, and the wicked from the righteous.

Part One is there to show you this: If you have trusted in Jesus Christ for your salvation, then God doesn't see you as disgusting and vile. He genuinely, actually, truly sees you as righteous. And if God Himself sees us a certain way, then how can we see ourselves otherwise?

Part Two explains the crucial truth that even though all sinners are equal before God, still "all sins are not equal."

On this foundation, with the understanding that it's appropriate to recognize wickedness and hypocrisy in the church, Part Three then gives you some tools to help you know how to discern and wisely expose these noxious elements.

Some of the teachers mentioned in this book have fallen out of favor because of some scandal or other. But when a building is built, it remains, even when the scaffolding falls away. It is the same with many of these false teachings. Even when the teachers themselves fall, you may not even realize how their false teachings have taken root in the church.

This book ends expanding on the topic with which I began: your righteousness. But after the background of Part Three has been laid, it goes into the topic even deeper. This right here, this joyful news about your righteousness in Jesus Christ, is the reason I began writing about these topics in the first place, even before I understood the world of spiritual abuse.

When you're exposing abuse, it's important to build on the Rock, not on the sand. That Solid-Rock foundation is offered to all of us in our Savior, the Lord Jesus Christ. We can find freedom and joy in Him.

PART ONE

God's Children Are Not Vile and Disgusting But Have Full Access to Joyful Righteousness

CHAPTER 1

Does God Need to "Look Through the Filter of Jesus" to See His Children?

The teaching

Have you heard about those "blood-colored glasses" God the Father supposedly puts on when He views His children?

It's supposed to be encouraging to hear that He sees His children through the filter of His Son Jesus Christ. I've seen Christians nearly come to tears when they talk about how God the Father is wearing "blood-colored glasses" to look at us, so that He can see the righteousness of His Son instead of our sinfulness.

So we are told, because of this He sees His blood-bought children as holy *instead of the unrighteous, filthy, utterly degraded, deceitfully wicked, totally sinful, vile creatures we actually are.*

I'd heard it all my life. (Yes, they were talking about the "blood-colored glasses" back in the 1960s and 70s too.) And I believed it.

The challenge

But there came a time, when I was immersed in the Word of God, that I questioned it. "If God sees us one way," I pondered, "but we are actually something quite different, doesn't that mean that God is deceiving Himself?"

Have you ever wondered this same thing?

I've sat on this question for years. A satisfactory answer has not been forthcoming, even as I continue to hear the "blood-colored glasses" teaching being taught.

The other problem with this teaching that has greatly troubled me is that it is nowhere taught in the Bible. In fact, the Bible teaches something radically different.

What does the Bible say about the children of God who are bought with the precious blood of Jesus Christ? Here are just a few statements of "how God sees" us, if you will, with the understanding that "how God sees us" is what is actually true about us.

- We are saints—holy ones (Ephesians 1:1 and other Pauline epistles).
- In the Holy Spirit we have direct access to God the Father (Ephesians 2:18).
- We are established, anointed, and sealed by God in Christ (2 Corinthians 1:21-22).
- We are seated in heavenly places with Christ (Ephesians 2:6).
- We are members of Christ's body (1 Corinthians 12:27).
- We are complete in Jesus Christ (Colossians 2:10).
- We are chosen of God, holy and dearly beloved (Colossians 3:12).
- We are new creations in Christ so that we can become the righteousness of God (2 Corinthians 5:17-21).
- We have been given great and precious promises by God, through which we can share in His nature (2 Peter 1:3-4).
- We have received abundant grace and the free gift of righteousness. We reign in life through Jesus Christ (Romans 5:17).
- We are more than conquerors through Him who loves us (Romans 8:37).

- ➢ We were washed, sanctified, justified in the name of the Lord Jesus Christ and by the Spirit of God (1 Corinthians 6:11).
- ➢ We are joint-heirs with Christ (Romans 8:17).
- ➢ We are united with the Lord and have become one spirit with Him (1 Corinthians 6:17).
- ➢ We are part of a chosen generation, a royal priesthood, a holy nation, a purchased people who have been called out of darkness into His marvelous light (1 Peter 2:9).

The truth

The fact is that when by faith we come into the family of God through Jesus Christ—that is, when we become true Christians—we are changed. We are no longer unrighteous—directed toward sin. We become righteous—directed toward God.

Not simply in name, but in actuality.

We are no longer filthy. We have been washed clean. We no longer have deceitful and desperately wicked hearts.[1] We have been given His truth and holiness. We are no longer vile. We are His beloved sons and daughters. We are no longer slaves to sin.

Through the Holy Spirit we have the power to joyfully say "no" to sin and joyfully say "yes" to God.

Does God have to look at us through the filter of His Son Jesus Christ? I offer a resounding no. The veil of the temple has been torn in two. There is no more division between us and God the Father. Now we can go boldly before the throne of grace, so that we may obtain mercy and find grace to help in time of need.[2]

Do we go in because of Jesus? Absolutely, no question about it.

---

[1] This is an allusion to Jeremiah 17:9, which tells us that the human heart is deceitful above all things and desperately wicked (or sick, depending on the translation). This Scripture is addressed in Book 3 of the *Untwisting Scriptures* series, *Your Words, Your Emotions*, p 113.

[2] Hebrews 4:16.

But do we go in with Jesus shielding and filtering so our vileness can't be observed by the Father?

No, that's not what the Scriptures teach.

> *Another, very similar teaching is the "robe of righteousness" teaching. This says that God clothes us in a robe of righteousness at conversion. This one IS mentioned in Scripture, but only in the Old Testament, in Isaiah 61:10 (KJV): "I will greatly rejoice in the LORD, my soul shall be joyful in my God; for he hath clothed me with the garments of salvation, he hath covered me with the robe of righteousness." . . .*
>
> *In the New Testament, however, righteousness is presented as something within us, instead of over top of us. My problem with the "robe of righteousness" idea is that we could be vile and filthy underneath the robe, but it would be "hiding" our sin—along the same lines as the "blood-colored glasses" idea.*[3]

The joy

Jesus Christ does not have to stand between us and God. Instead, through the power of His death (taking our sins upon Himself) and resurrection (rising in victory over sin), we are fully received as His beloved sons and daughters. Because of Jesus, we are filled with His righteousness. When you are His son or daughter, you have access to so much. And what's more,

**By faith you can expect transformation
in the very areas where you feel the weakest
in your love for God and others.**

For example, do you feel a hard place in your heart toward a certain category of people, as I did toward those with extreme chronic physical illnesses? (I knew this was because someone in

---

[3] Joel Horst, comment on https://heresthejoy.com/2019/10/heres-whats-wrong-with-god-looking-through-the-filter-of-jesus-to-see-his-children/#comment-201515. Joel writes at www.joelhorst.com.

CHAPTER 1 – DOES GOD NEED TO LOOK THROUGH THE "FILTER" OF JESUS?

my life had used chronic physical illnesses to manipulate and control me and others, but I still felt great distress when I realized I had it.) Then you can ask Him to change it and by faith expect that He will.[4] In fact, years ago when I asked God to change that particular hard place in my heart, I was excited to anticipate how in the world He was going to do it. It felt like it would be a miracle, because it seemed like such an impossibly hard place.

For me, my transformation in this particular area came specifically through understanding how trauma affects people physically, to fill me with compassion—yes, even compassion for the manipulative and controlling person in my life.[5]

And I stood in awe of the work of God in the very area in which I had asked Him to work.

Ultimately, it comes down to identity—am I a ransomed, redeemed, transformed child of God, or am I a groveling servant who is unworthy of even a crumb of God's attention?

> *I feel rather passionate about all this, because it changed my life when I realized that Jesus didn't just do an external work from the outside in–He completely changed me on the inside and is continuing to do so! I have experienced so much freedom from learning to walk in the reality of being innately righteous instead of a sinner who struggles to do the right thing.*[6]

Here's the joy for the people of God. Through Jesus Christ, there is great joy in knowing that not only are we "seen" as righteous and holy, but that God the Father is not playing mind games

---

[4] I believe it is a devilish teaching from Bill Gothard and others that we should never have any expectations. See "What Can We Expect from God?" *Here's the Joy,* July 20, 2022. https://heresthejoy.com/2022/07/what-can-we-expect-from-god/

[5] Relationship parameters in the case of this controlling family member were still appropriate. I talk more about that in the article, "Jesus Didn't Have Boundaries, So I Shouldn't Either," *Here's the Joy,* January 31, 2022, https://heresthejoy.com/2022/01/jesus-didnt-have-boundaries-so-i-shouldnt-either.

[6] Joel Horst, comment on https://heresthejoy.com/2019/10/heres-whats-wrong-with-god-looking-through-the-filter-of-jesus-to-see-his-children/#comment-201515.

with Himself to do so. Because we actually *are* righteous and holy. He expects us, by faith, to learn what that means.

> *I always found it very distancing to hear that when God looked at me he saw Jesus. Like most people, I believe the deepest desire of my heart is to be known and loved by God, for who I am.*
>
> *So many of Satan's deceptions involve conflating doctrine and religion with relationship. I believe that Jesus came to show us the 'Abba' way, which invites us to come to God as little children, confident in his desire to shower us with his love.*[7]

Here's the joy for the people of God. When we see a need for change in our lives having to do with love toward God and others, by faith we can *expect* Him to change it. He delights to do this for His beloved sons and daughters.

This is the way God sees us. This is how God loves us. This is how the Holy Spirit works in us.

This is good news.

UNTWISTED TRUTH FROM CHAPTER 1

- ❖ God does not need to look through the "filter" of His Son Jesus Christ to look at His children.
- ❖ His children are holy, righteous, and clean rather than tainted, wicked, and stained.
- ❖ Because of what the Lord Jesus Christ has done for us, we can go boldly before the throne of God the Father.
- ❖ By faith we can expect our Lord to continue to transform us in the areas of our spirit, even the areas where we feel the greatest need.

---

[7] TS00, comment on https://heresthejoy.com/2019/10/heres-whats-wrong-with-god-looking-through-the-filter-of-jesus-to-see-his-children/#comment-201511

CHAPTER 2

Are You the Prodigal Son or the Older Brother?

The teaching

The prodigal son and the older brother are characters in a parable Jesus told in Luke 15. The prodigal son got his inheritance early, left home, spent it all in debauchery, and ended up in a pig sty. He came to his senses and made his way home into the arms of a loving father who fully forgave him and welcomed him with a feast.

The older brother was the outwardly faithful one who stayed home and did all the things he was supposed to do. He became angry that he didn't get a feast when he had been such a good rule-follower.

Of course it's clear that these two brothers were both in their own way self-centered and missing relationship. (Except that the prodigal returned to relationship, and the older brother didn't.)

Often when this parable is preached, the audience is challenged that each one of us is either the rebellious one, running away from the loving Father who is waiting for us, or the self-justified, self-righteous one who feels above sin and points the finger at others.

The common teaching is if you're not like the younger brother and wandering away, you're like the older brother and serving out of hope of reward rather than out of relationship. The message you receive may strongly imply that throughout your life you'll be doomed to slog through either "rebellious sin" or "religious sin" and that you must be very thankful for the forgiveness the cross of Christ offers you for your constant violations of God's holiness.[1]

So which one are you?

The challenge

That was a trick question, of course. In the teaching of logic it's called a false dilemma. Because you really don't have to be either one.

You do not need to be stuck in the ghastly mire of either-ever-wandering-prodigal-or-self-righteous-older-brother.

There is a Living God of love and power.

There is a Loving Savior who has power over sin.

There is a Holy Spirit full of power to live in victory.

There is great power available to you to live in joyful pursuit of the things of eternal importance.

The truth

This parable of Jesus wasn't even about the power (or not) to live the Christian life. It was about which group of people would come into lasting relationship with the Father: the immoral Gentiles or the rule-following Jews.

The point of the story was that the invitation of the Father was wide open to both—*come into lasting relationship.*

---

[1] More on this in chapter 16.

And thus, the first churches consisted of both those who had lived in utter licentiousness having never known of the prophecies of Messiah (the Gentiles), as well as those who had followed the rules all their lives, having heard about Messiah for generation after generation (the Jews). It was a beautiful, incredible sight to behold.

"Come into lasting relationship with the Father!" Jesus invited the Jews who were listening to His parable. "The Father is calling rule followers as well as profligate prodigals. Come!"

How shall we live after entering that lasting relationship?

The parable doesn't talk about that. It isn't what it was about.

Jesus wasn't talking to Christians.

How sad that some are left with the feeling that even after they come to Jesus like a returning prodigal, they're still doomed to be judgmental, self-righteous, and pharisaical. . . .

There is a better way, friends.

The joy

Picture the younger brother being filled with love for his father, wanting always to honor him in everything simply because he loves him. Picture the older brother turning from his selfishness to rejoice in his younger sibling's return and then living in perpetual relationship with his father.

Picture the Father having the power to infuse His two sons, as they make request of Him, to turn their hearts toward truth and right, toward goodness and love and mercy.

This is the power that is available to us.

I'm not talking about living a life that is completely sinless and flawless. There will still be distractions and sins to be overcome. I'm certainly not saying there won't be past trauma that needs to be worked through. I'm talking about how we don't have to live in the half-life of Romans 7,[2] with self-centered idolatry at our very core. Instead,

> **At the core of our being
> we can look to Him in faith to be changed,
> as Romans 8 and other Scriptures describe,
> to love Him and walk in His Spirit
> through the resurrection power of our Savior Jesus.**

Yes, and Yes... I have been both the prodigal and the elder brother in heart at times (whether ignorantly, comfortably, or conveniently). I see the reductionist black or white thinking, and know it is not the only choice. Thankful God meets us and walks with us, away from ourselves, toward Himself in relationship. In both cases, it was about relationship with the Father. And a relationship with the Father changes everything. "But the path of the just (righteous) is as the shining light, That shineth more and more unto the perfect day." Proverbs 4:18 (KJV)[3]

In this new life will you be mired in self-righteousness, so that you look down on others? No, you will have the heart of Jesus, the heart of the Father for others. You'll have a growing desire to reach out to others with His love.

The way Jesus told His story, the punchline was left hanging. The older brother was invited into relationship with the Father, but we were left not knowing if the older brother would follow through. As it turned out, the majority of the Jews (the rule-followers that the older brother represented) turned on Jesus and slaughtered Him, even in the name of the rules they purported to follow.

---

[2] "The Trump Card of Romans 7," *Here's the Joy*, May 20, 2012, https://heresthejoy.com/2012/05/the-trump-card-of-romans-7

[3] Susan Brinley, comment on https://heresthejoy.com/2018/07/are-you-the-prodigal-son-or-the-older-brother-2/#comment-192014

CHAPTER 2 – ARE YOU THE PRODIGAL SON OR THE OLDER BROTHER?

Why are so many people who call themselves Christians so hateful? I can see only two possibilities. They have never come into lasting relationship with the Father. (And so I would say they're not real Christians.) Or they have been told that they are the older brother and that there is no higher level to which to rise.

That way of thinking does not end well.

But for anyone who does truly come into lasting relationship, there is great hope. There's a world of beauty to explore when it comes to learning to live life in the Spirit.

Rather than being stuck in "prodigal son" or "older brother," it is available to all of us to come into relationship with the Father, being transformed in Him, to love Him and love others by the power of Jesus Christ.

UNTWISTED TRUTH FROM CHAPTER 2

❖ The parable of the prodigal son isn't about you as a believer being one son or the other. It is about both Gentiles and Jews being invited into lasting relationship with a good and loving Father.

❖ Transformed, lasting relationship with the Heavenly Father is available to all who come to Him in faith.

CHAPTER 3

Nothing Like The Sheep Sermon to Make You Feel Stupid, Disgusting, and Useless

The teaching

Not long ago I visited a church where I got to hear The Sheep Sermon again. It had been quite a while, years I guess. But The Sheep Sermon hadn't changed much over the years. It even still had the part about the broken leg.

You may have heard some version of it, but this version started with Isaiah 53:6.

> *All we like sheep have gone astray;*
> *We have turned—every one—to his own way,*
> *And the Lord has laid on Him*
> *The iniquity of us all.*

I noticed that the preacher assumed that the "we" referred to us Christians. He also assumed that the "have gone" means presently, right now. Then he proceeded to spend a very long time telling us what sheep are like, the essence of which boiled down to his three points:

- Sheep are dumb.
- Sheep are defenseless.
- Sheep are directionless.

The way he described how filthy sheep can be was at times even disgusting, so I thought maybe there should have been a fourth point:

- Sheep are disgusting.

He then applied his points to us, the Christians sitting under him right at that time, and told us:

> We are dumb.
> We are directionless.
> We are defenseless.

Then he told us that God would take care of us by being a Provider, a Protector, and another P word that I failed to jot down. (Maybe you've heard The Sheep Sermon too so you can let me know what it was.)

If you haven't been initiated into The Sheep Sermon, you may wonder what the part was about the broken leg.

The preacher said just like a shepherd might have to break the leg of a wandering sheep, so the Great Shepherd, God, might have to break our legs—bring bad things into our lives—in order to get us to obey Him and follow Him. Of course then the sheep would be useless, at least for a time.

Don't check behind the curtain to see that there's no mention of this in the Bible. Also, real-life shepherds never do it.

As it turned out, this preacher didn't mention Jesus and how He took the iniquity of us all, I guess because he ran out of time since he had spent so long telling us all the disgusting details about sheep and that long story about a man getting a traffic ticket (the point of which I never did quite understand).

So . . . .

CHAPTER 3 –THE SHEEP SERMON TO MAKE YOU FEEL STUPID, DISGUSTING, & USELESS

The challenge

For anyone who has ever heard The Sheep Sermon, which was probably more or less like that one (except perhaps for the part about the traffic ticket), I'd like to talk about sheep. And shepherds. And who Christians really are.

First, consider the context of Isaiah 53, the chapter from which that verse was taken. *The entire chapter is about Jesus.* He is the one who has borne our griefs and carried our sorrows, who was pierced for our transgressions and crushed for our iniquities. He is the one who went to the slaughter like a silent lamb, for us all.

And in the middle of this description of our suffering Savior, Isaiah refers to the ones for whom Jesus died:

All we like sheep have gone astray.
We have turned every one to his own way.

This is a description of sheep without a shepherd.

Christians, those who are in Christ, who have trusted in Jesus Christ for their full righteousness, those who partake fully of the New Covenant in the blood of Jesus Christ, *count this as part of their past, not their present.*

The way sheep are described in the New Covenant of Jesus Christ, let's see how negative it is.

In John 10 Jesus told how He is the true Shepherd, the Good Shepherd. He calls His sheep by name and leads them out and they follow Him, because they know His voice. He said they won't listen to the voice of a stranger or a thief. He said He would lay down His life for His sheep, not like the robber, who would only steal, kill, and destroy. He emphasized that He and His sheep *know each other.*

In Matthew 10:16 Jesus sent the disciples out like sheep in the midst of wolves and told them to be wise as serpents and innocent as doves.

In Luke 12:32 He said,

*Fear not little flock,
for it is your Father's good pleasure to give you the kingdom.*

Peter wrote in 1 Peter 2:25

*For you [the Christians Peter was writing to]
were straying like sheep,
but have now returned to the Shepherd and Overseer of your souls.*

In 1 Peter 5:2-3 Peter wrote to the church elders,

*Shepherd the flock of God that is among you,
exercising oversight, not under compulsion, but willingly,
as God would have you; not for shameful gain, but eagerly;
not domineering over those in your charge,
but being examples to the flock.*

And of course we don't want to miss perhaps the most obvious one: In Luke 15 Jesus told the parable of the lost sheep that the faithful shepherd went to find. (No broken legs included!)

I remember at least once sitting in junior church or Sunday school as a young child and hearing a lesson of the shepherd going after the sheep and rescuing it and bringing it back and breaking its leg. . . . Never stopped to check scripture to find that it was not ever part of the story. It was upsetting to me then, and it still is. A lot of incorrect teaching can lead to very bad theology that affects our living.[1]

The truth

These are truly beautiful and encouraging Scriptures, especially the lengthy description in John 10. Our Lord Jesus makes it really clear that:

---

[1] Lydia St. Louis, comment on https://heresthejoy.com/2017/09/nothing-like-the-sheep-sermon-to-make-you-feel-stupid-disgusting-and-useless/#comment-189610.

CHAPTER 3 – THE SHEEP SERMON TO MAKE YOU FEEL STUPID, DISGUSTING, & USELESS

- *His sheep are not dumb.* They know His voice. They're able to distinguish His voice from that of a stranger.
- *His sheep are not directionless.* They follow the Good Shepherd.
- *His sheep are not defenseless.* Jesus is "the door of the sheep," which means a predator wanting to steal the sheep would have to go through Jesus first.

And furthermore, I just have to add:

- *His sheep are not disgusting.* We are washed clean in the blood of the Lamb and stand in honor before the King of Kings.

There are plenty of other metaphors in the New Testament for the New Covenant people of God. Christian believers are called the *temple* (1 Corinthians 6:19), *priests* (1 Peter 2:5), *children and heirs of God* (Galatians 3:29, Romans 8:17), *the body of Christ* (1 Corinthians 12:27), *warriors of God* (Ephesians 6:10-18), *jars of clay* holding precious treasure (2 Corinthians 4:7), *fountains of living water* (John 7:37-39), and many other things. Each image is designed to communicate an important truth.

The important truth about being a New Covenant sheep is that His sheep are His beloved flock. We know His voice. We are not directionless. We follow Him.

And not only are the people of Christ not dumb, because we know His voice, but when you look at other parts of the New Covenant, you see, for example, that Jesus Christ is made unto us wisdom in 1 Corinthians 1:30. James tells us if we lack wisdom we can seek it from God and expect Him to give it to us. James 3 assumes that there will be **wise** and understanding Christians in the church.

God's people have everything they need at their disposal to be the opposite of dumb.

And not only are the flock of Christ not defenseless (because He is the door of the sheep), but in Ephesians 6 when we're told to take all the armor of God, we're given the means of protection against all the fiery darts of the enemy. And not only that, but we're given two offensive weapons, the sword of the Spirit which is the Word of God, and the weapon of all-prayer, by which we go forward in the power of the Holy Spirit against the enemy. No, *we are not defenseless.*

The preacher I heard was describing sheep without a shepherd. But that is not who we are. In fact, in Matthew 9:36 when Jesus looked on people and felt compassion for them because He saw them as sheep without a shepherd, *it was the people who didn't know Him.*

The joy

Here's the joy for the people of God: you don't have to live your life under the dark cloud of thinking you're dumb, directionless, and defenseless like a flock of disgusting sheep (who are so stubborn in their straying that they'll probably need to get their legs broken).

Instead, if you are in Christ . . .

- ➢ You are part of the precious flock of Jesus, and you recognize His voice.
- ➢ You follow Him where He leads.
- ➢ You are called to be a warrior of God, and you are equipped to be protected and even to fight in the power of the Holy Spirit.

> *My deepest fears have demanded an answer for how I know I won't become the most evil things I've witnessed and experienced, in part due to an environment that said my sin was as bad as my abuser's and I was just as fallen (although I was a believer). I've taken immense comfort in the truth that God keeps his sheep. He restores. He renews. He works to guard us in so many ways:*

conscience, companionship of other believers, His word, His Spirit. We are not moving from evil to evil, or EVEN from goodness to evil. We are moving from glory to glory.[2]

Here's the joy for those who have trusted in Christ: We don't have to take The Sheep Sermon as true of us just because it's true of sheep without a shepherd.

We not only have the perfect Shepherd; we also have the perfect armor: the armor of God. We have the Holy Spirit dwelling in these jars of clay, springing out of these fountains, as we continually come to Jesus Christ.

We are not stupid. We are not disgusting. We are not useless or directionless or defenseless. We have a Good Shepherd in Jesus Christ. We know Him and can follow Him, and even more, we can be confident that by the Spirit of the living God we can be filled with His power and authority against the enemy.

Not only is there much to be grateful for. There is also much life to be lived.

UNTWISTED TRUTH FROM CHAPTER 3

- ❖ "All we like sheep have gone astray" does not apply in the present to those who know the Lord Jesus Christ. It is about sheep without a shepherd.

- ❖ The New Testament uses many other metaphors for the people of God, all of which show a certain important attribute of His people.

- ❖ The sheep in the flock of our Lord Jesus Christ are not dumb, directionless, defenseless, or disgusting. Rather, they know and are known by and are protected by their Good Shepherd.

---

[2] Rhoda Hostetler, personal correspondence, June 25, 2022. Used by permission.

PART TWO

We Can Recognize and Reject Sin Leveling

CHAPTER 4

What is "Sin Leveling" and What's Wrong With It?

How "the equality of sin" is often presented

In conversation

I often write about spiritual abuse, in social media, on my website, on my Untwisting Scriptures Facebook page, and in groups. Sometimes I name the wolves in sheep's clothing. When I said something on social media about a popular celebrity who was accused of rape by thirty women,[1] I received this comment:

> Along with all this, let us who hate what is done as this subject reveals, remember how our God hates all wrongs of our hidden hearts.

This is an example of what we call "sin leveling": treating all sins as equal.

When you point out the serial rapist's sin, the sin levelers say, you need to point at your own sin too, because God hates the rapist's sin, and *God hates your hidden sin.*

---

[1] Eventually 60 women came forward. Patrick Ryan, Maria Puente, and Carly Mallenbaum, "A complete list of the 60 Bill Cosby accusers and their reactions to his prison sentence," *USA Today,* April 27, 2018. https://www.usatoday.com/story/life/people/2018/04/27/bill-cosby-full-list-accusers/555144002/

Well, but doesn't He? And does it make you think you need to stop talking about the sins of others? Does it leave you confused? This kind of teaching left one reader of mine in agony:

I used to worry so much about the unseen sin in me. I believed what the experts taught about our sin nature making us filthy rags, disgusting to look upon, a major disappointment to God. I would search my heart looking for the sin and evil in me. But how could I confess stuff I didn't know I was guilty of committing? I was trying so hard to do everything I was taught, but it was a no-win situation. It left me feeling defeated and without any hope for resolution— I was filthy and guilty inside because of "hidden" sin I hadn't confessed or eradicated.[2]

I've also written on social media about how some sins are worse than others—what this very section is about. I would then often receive statements like this one:

> As Christians we are taught that every sin is equally heinous in the eyes of God. . . . Sin is sin. I see absolutely no hierarchy. No one sin is worse than another. They all are a mark of the depraved nature of man apart from God.

It is a revealing statement. But is it correct?

In formal teaching

Here are just a few examples of this teaching from current popular books published by major Christian publishers.

> Unlike our legal system, sins are not weighted by their seriousness. There are no misdemeanors in the realm of sin. Sin is sin, and it is serious because of what it does to the soul.[3]

---

[2] Alison Anderson, comment on https://heresthejoy.com/2019/10/heres-whats-wrong-with-god-looking-through-the-filter-of-jesus-to-see-his-children/#comment-201537

[3] John Ortberg, *Soul Keeping: Caring for the Most Important Part of You*, Zondervan, 2014, p 72.

CHAPTER 4 – WHAT IS "SIN LEVELING" AND WHAT'S WRONG WITH IT?

> Nowhere in the Bible, however, do we find God distinguishing between levels of sin. God doesn't share our rating system [small, medium, and large sins]. To him, all sin is equally evil, and all sinners are equally lovable. . . . God just calls sin, sin.[4]

> I think all sins are equal because anything that distracts us from God's purpose for our lives has the same result: we're missing out on God's purpose for our lives. He's designed us for a special, perfect thing, and when we choose anything other than that, we miss it. The specifics of why we missed it probably matter less than we think. What we missed is what matters. God's big, crazy gift of love goes unclaimed for another hour . . . another day . . . another year. Whether you decided to ignore it because you were chasing money or girls or pie or a million other things isn't the point. You missed the gift, and that's what God cares about. You missed another day for him to let you know how much he loves you and how important you are.
>
> That's why, even if we don't believe it sometimes, I think all sins are equal.[5]

> The truth is, I am Zacchaeus. I may not be short in stature, but I'm short spiritually, in my own ability and my own capacity. Even if I want to get to Jesus, even if I want to see Jesus, I can't see past myself. I can't see past my sin, past my distractions, past my ego.[6]

And so even those who are trying to recover from great evils such as sex trafficking and being used for child pornography, being

---

[4] Judah Smith, *Jesus Is: Find a New Way to Be Human,* Thomas Nelson, 2013, pp 4-5.
[5] Jonathan Acuff, *Stuff Christians Like,* Zondervan, 2010, pp 248-249.
[6] Judah Smith, *Jesus Is,* p 10.

enslaved on a concentration camp that fronts as a "home for boys," being used as the "living sacrifice" in satanic ritual abuse . . . still they hear something along these lines (a compilation of many similar teachings) . . .

> The very fact that you're talking about someone else's sin shows that you're proud.[7] We're all desperately wicked. Judge not, that ye be not judged. You should just be talking about your own sin. You're the worst sinner you know. All Christians are hypocrites. How dare you judge! He may have a speck in his eye, but you have a beam in yours.

> We're all Pharisees of one sort or another, you see. That's why we resist the gospel which tells us that "While we were still helpless, at the right time Christ died for [us]."[8]

This author is doing that thing again, that thing where teachers talk to Christians as if they're not Christians. It's all too common, and it can serve to twist clear Scriptures into something ghastly.

Christians have not resisted the gospel! By definition, Christians have embraced the gospel. We've rejoiced in the fact that Jesus Christ died for us at exactly the right time.

> Sometimes I wonder if in our quest to purify the church, we've become more like Pharisees than like Jesus. Accidental Pharisees perhaps. But Pharisees nonetheless.[9]

---

[7] And bitter, and not giving up your rights, and taking up offenses, as I talk about in the first *Untwisting Scriptures* book. And disobedient and rebellious, not submitting to authority, discontent, and not staying under your umbrella of authority, as I talk about in the second *Untwisting Scriptures* book. And gossiping, bearing false witness, sinfully offended, slandering, tearing down, and sinning through your emotions, as I address in the third *Untwisting Scriptures* book.

[8] Fleming Rutledge, *Not Ashamed of the Gospel: Sermons from Paul's Letter to the Romans*, Eerdmans, 2007, p 144-145. The Scripture quoted is Romans 5:6.

[9] Larry Osborne, *Accidental Pharisees: Avoiding Pride, Exclusivity, and the Other Dangers of Overzealous Faith*, Zondervan, 2012, p 37.

This is sin leveling. The crimes of the Pharisees were great. Some of them, like Paul, became Pharisees because that was all they had known,[10] but none of the ones Jesus rebuked had actually put their faith and trust in Him. This statement once again treats Christians like non-Christians.

Yes, Christians can have unseen sins and blind spots. Yes, true Christians can be immature and have growing to do. Yes, true Christians can even experience grave battles against sin. But no true Christian is going to live the double life the Pharisees lived.[11]

Thomas Aquinas, the Father of Sin Leveling

A special nod to medieval monk Thomas Aquinas who probably did more to promote the teaching of "sin equality" than anyone else, considering how great his influence was. Thomas Aquinas was a Medieval Catholic monk who helped root out the heretic Protestants, so it is surprising to me how deeply his teaching on the equality of sin took hold among the Protestants. (I've wondered if it was because it can be used as a tool of control, but I cannot say for sure.)

In his book *On Evil,* Aquinas listed 18 reasons he concluded that sins are equal (some of which were redundant).[12] With all his arguments, though, he gave only two Scriptures, which I'm addressing here.

Some Scriptures used to support sin leveling

Certain sin-leveling teachings I'll confront in upcoming chapters. But here are a few more.

---

[10] 1 Timothy 1:12.

[11] More on that in chapter 8.

[12] Thomas Aquinas, *On Evil,* Oxford University Press, 2003, pp 124-127.

James 2:10

This is by far the most common one. Someone told me that because God is too holy to look upon sin, to Him, stealing a nickel is as loathsome a sin as murder. She used this verse as her support. Here it is in context.

> *If you really fulfill the royal law according to the Scripture, "You shall love your neighbor as yourself," you are doing well. But if you show partiality, you are committing sin and are convicted by the law as transgressors.* **For whoever keeps the whole law but fails in one point has become guilty of all of it.**

But James is not saying that each sin is equal to every other sin before God, any more than he's saying that each law is equal to every other law. After all, our Lord Jesus spoke about how some matters of the law (justice, mercy, and truth) are "weightier" than others.[13] He also pointed out that there are two laws that are greater than all the others and on which all the others hang.[14]

Instead, James is saying that each breaking of the law is enough to cut a person off from God. All will separate us from God, but not all are equally *heinous*.

On this point, I agree with the teachings of the Westminster Larger Catechism, teachings that are reflected in the laws of any just nation.

Q 151. Are all transgressions of the law of God equally heinous in themselves, and in the sight of God?

A. All transgressions of the law are not equally heinous; but some sins in themselves, and by reason of several aggravations, are more heinous in the sight of God than others. The "aggravations" include aspects of

---

[13] Matthew 23:23.
[14] Matthew 22:36-40.

CHAPTER 4 – WHAT IS "SIN LEVELING" AND WHAT'S WRONG WITH IT?

> ➢ The person committing the offense (perceived maturity, office held, etc.).
> ➢ The person against whom the offense has been committed (if it is God or man, if it is a "weak brother," etc. [I would add the obvious, "if it is a child"]).
> ➢ The offense (whether done in the heart alone or also in the actions; whether done in full understanding of the wrongness of the action; whether done deliberately and willfully and maliciously, etc.).
> ➢ The circumstances of the offense.[15]

Luke 16:10

Of the two Scriptures Thomas Aquinas used in his sin-leveling arguments, one was James 2:10, above. The other was Luke 16:10. About this Scripture, Aquinas said,

> If one sin is more serious than another, then a sin committed in a greater matter would be more serious than a sin committed in a lesser matter. For example, such would be the case if one should say that stealing a large amount of something is a more serious sin than to steal a little amount.
> But this is not true, since one who commits a lesser sin would also as a result commit a greater sin. For Luke 16:10 says: "One who is unjust in little things is unjust in greater things." Therefore one sin is not more serious than another.[16]

This argument, even though it's coming from a respected Medieval scholar, seems almost laughable to me. Here is the brief context of Jesus' statement:

---

[15] Westminster Larger Catechism, Question 151. https://thewestminsterstandard.org/westminster-larger-catechism/#151

[16] Thomas Aquinas, *On Evil*, p 125.

One who is faithful in a very little is also faithful in much,
*and **one who is dishonest in a very little is also dishonest in much.***
If then you have not been faithful in the unrighteous wealth,
who will entrust to you the true riches?

Jesus was simply talking about whether or not people are trustworthy. He was saying that as we observe people being faithful or unfaithful in the little things, we'll learn whether we can trust them in the big things. This is not about all sins being basically the same.

John 8:7

Let him who is without sin among you
be the first to throw a stone at her.

The argument goes like this: You have sin too, so you are not in a place to say anything about anyone else's sins.

The context of this oft-quoted verse is that the Pharisees, the proud and arrogant, wealthy and powerful religious leaders of Israel, brought out a woman who had been taken in adultery (while ignoring the man who had also participated). Pointing to the woman lying on the ground anticipating their impending blows, the proud and powerful ones challenged Jesus. "The law says we should stone her to death. What do you say?"

Jesus replied with the words above, challenging the proud and powerful to examine their own hearts.

Unless you're planning to kill a law-breaker with your own hands, you're in a different place from the Pharisees. Do you claim to be sinless? Do you plan to take the law into your own hands? Are you willing to examine your own heart?

When you cry out for other Christians to recognize the evils that are going on under their noses, this is not casting stones.

When you're calling for Christians to stop blaming and shaming victims of atrocious crimes, this is not casting stones.

When you call out for wicked hypocrites to be exposed, this is not casting stones. Rather than stone-casting, you're seeking to shine a light into some very dark places.

Anti-sin-leveling Scriptures

Certain statements in the Scriptures make it surprisingly clear that some sins are worse than others.

From the teachings of Jesus

Luke 12:47-48 says,

> *And that servant who knew his master's will*
> *but did not get ready or act according to his will,*
> *will receive a severe beating.*
> *But the one who did not know, and did what deserved a beating,*
> *will receive a light beating.*
> *Everyone to whom much was given, of him much will be required,*
> *and from him to whom they entrusted much,*
> *they will demand the more.*

Jesus said that the punishment of those who did understand what the master required would be more severe than the punishment of those who did not understand. The sin of disobeying when you know the full extent of the disobedience is worse than the sin of disobeying when you don't know the full extent of it. Clearly one sin is worse than the other.

The sin of Pilate compared to the sin of the Pharisees

Pilate, who condemned Jesus to death, didn't understand what was going on. But the scribes, Pharisees, and lawyers understood full well what they were doing. For this reason, Jesus said in John 19:11,

> *he who delivered me over to you* **has the greater sin.**

From Matthew Henry:

> *Yet theirs [their sin] that delivered him to Pilate was the greater sin. By this it appears that all sins are not equal, but some more heinous than others; some comparatively as gnats, others as camels; some as motes in the eyes, others as beams; some as pence, others as pounds.*[17]

From the teachings of the apostles

The apostles were not sinless. We know that Peter sinned quite egregiously, for example, because Paul called him out and even wrote about him for all of us to read about thousands of years later.[18] And yet, in Acts 2:14-40, Peter had no problem at all calling out the great sin of the Jewish religious leaders who were responsible for the death of Jesus. In fact, the way he spoke to them bore remarkable similarities to the way Jesus had spoken to the same group of people.

How can that be, if all sins are equal? He shouldn't have "cast stones," should he? He shouldn't have pointed the finger of judgment, should he?

Peter's boldness in calling out sin can only be because he knew it was appropriate for one who was right with God to call out the heinous crimes of those who had violated His Son, the perfectly innocent one.

No one is as perfectly innocent as our Lord Jesus, but there are other innocents when it comes to sin.

> *I was abused as a toddler. Part of the response was to rebuke me for not being a modest enough toddler.*
>
> *I found immense comfort from Proverbs 17:15. "The one who acquits the guilty and the one who condemns the innocent—both of them are an abomination to the Lord." (NET)*

---

[17] Matthew Henry, commentary on John 19, *Bible Study Tools*, http://www.biblestudytools.com/commentaries/matthew-henry-complete/john/19.html

[18] Galatians 2:11-21.

CHAPTER 4 – WHAT IS "SIN LEVELING" AND WHAT'S WRONG WITH IT?

> *As I told a friend this, he sincerely urged me to remember that I WAS a sinner. He loves me. I don't doubt his sincerity. But the strength of sin-leveling teaching overcame both his love for me and his common sense.*
>
> *But in that case, I was not the sinner. In that case, I was the innocent.*[19]

It's time to dismantle all the "sin leveling" teaching that is circulating in our churches.

It's time to be able to recognize that all sins are not equal.

UNTWISTED TRUTH FROM CHAPTER 4

- ❖ The Scriptures do not treat all sins as equal.
- ❖ Christians, by definition, have not resisted the gospel but have embraced it. It is appropriate to distinguish them, in writing and speaking, from those with hard hearts toward the Lord.
- ❖ Certain Scriptures used to support sin leveling actually mean something quite different when considered in context.
- ❖ Certain Scriptures make it very clear that all sins are not equal.

---

[19] Anonymous, personal correspondence, June 23, 2022. Used by permission.

CHAPTER 5

Pronoun Trouble in Romans 2 That Can Keep the Oppressed in a Place of Bondage

Not long ago I received a request from a reader to help her understand the first verse of Romans 2 as it might apply to praying for God's judgment against one's wicked abuser:

Therefore you have no excuse, O man, every one of you who judges. For in passing judgment on another you condemn yourself, because you, the judge, practice the very same things.

She told me that because of this Scripture in particular, someone she knew had refrained from naming her abuser's actions as wicked, and had thus continued for a long time to be in a dangerous relationship.

So here is a modified version of my reply.

~~~

Dear friend,

Three important points to consider

First of all, your question brings up the issue of Pronoun Trouble. I was taught, either implicitly or explicitly, that wherever I

45

read a pronoun in Scripture, I should insert my own name and identity. Then—unless it's painfully obvious it doesn't fit—I should apply the statement to myself.[1]

I accepted this teaching as true and part of the way the Bible "comes alive" to me. That is, until sometime in the 1990s, when I received the challenge that this method of interpretation was not only incorrect but potentially downright detrimental to our understanding of God and His Kingdom.

At first this challenge almost upended my world, but ultimately it revolutionized my Bible study.

So, that to say, I'm working from the hermeneutical understanding that when you read a pronoun, it doesn't apply to you. I mean, *maybe* it does, but first of all, it applies to someone else, the person or people it's being written to. Then, if you're in the same category as that person, then it applies to you. Otherwise it doesn't. As my husband has observed, "When we read the epistles, we're reading over someone else's shoulder."

Second, it's important to remember that Scripture is to be read like any other literary work, in that each book should be taken as a whole to be understood. I know it's considered normal and expected to take verses out of context ever since the advent of verse separators. But the book of Romans is one gigantic argument, and if one verse is pulled out of context, it can be misunderstood.

Not only is Paul speaking to a specific group encompassed in that "O man" address at the beginning of Romans 2, but also he's working his way through an argument that started back at the beginning of Romans 1.

And finally, I believe there is overwhelming Scriptural (not to mention logical) evidence that treating all sins as equal—that is, sin leveling—is extremely harmful to the body of Christ.

---

[1] See more at "'Pronoun Trouble' in Galatians 5:16-17," *Here's the Joy*, December 12, 2010. https://heresthejoy.com/2010/12/pronoun-trouble-in-galatians-516-17

I believe those three truths are foundational to understanding this Scripture. So now I'll proceed with my interpretation of the passage.

Working our way through the passage

When you first start reading Romans 2, it might not be quite clear who the "O man" is at the beginning of the chapter. This is because we don't immediately assume it's "me," considering the Rule of Scriptural Pronouns that says the pronouns refer primarily to the person being written to at the time rather than the modern-day reader.

The person Paul was writing to becomes clear as you proceed through the chapter.

So, imagine one of the Christians in Rome receiving this letter from Paul. Then he takes it to a Jewish gathering place and begins reading at Romans 1:18-32.

It's familiar to us now, but imagine a Jew in the public square hearing it for the first time.

*For the **wrath of God** is revealed from heaven*
***against all ungodliness and unrighteousness** of men,*
who by their unrighteousness suppress the truth.
For what can be known about God is plain to them,
because God has shown it to them.
For his invisible attributes, namely, his eternal power
and divine nature, have been clearly perceived,
ever since the creation of the world,
in the things that have been made.
*So **they are without excuse**.*
*For although they knew God, **they did not honor him as God***
or give thanks to him, but they became futile in their thinking,
and their foolish hearts were darkened.
Claiming to be wise, they became fools,
and exchanged the glory of the immortal God for images
resembling mortal man and birds and animals and creeping things.

> *Therefore **God gave them up***
> *in the lusts of their hearts to impurity,*
> *to the dishonoring of their bodies among themselves,*
> *because they exchanged the truth about God for a lie*
> *and worshiped and served the creature rather than the Creator,*
> *who is blessed forever! Amen.*
> *For this reason **God gave them up** to dishonorable passions.*
> *For their women exchanged natural relations*
> *for those that are contrary to nature;*
> *and the men likewise gave up natural relations with women*
> *and were consumed with passion for one another,*
> *men committing shameless acts with men*
> *and receiving in themselves the due penalty for their error.*
> *And since they did not see fit to acknowledge God,*
> ***God gave them up** to a debased mind*
> *to do what ought not to be done.*
> *They were filled with all manner of unrighteousness, evil,*
> *covetousness, malice.*
> *They are full of envy, murder, strife, deceit, maliciousness.*
> *They are gossips, slanderers, haters of God, insolent, haughty,*
> *boastful, inventors of evil, disobedient to parents, foolish,*
> *faithless, heartless, ruthless.*
> *Though **they know God's righteous decree***
> ***that those who practice such things deserve to die,***
> *they not only do them but give approval to those who practice them.*

Imagine how a typical first-century Jew might respond. "Well, yes, of course those heathen pagan Gentiles are condemned. That was never in question. Yes, absolutely. This all applies to them."

Then, imagine that the letter-reader turns around and faces his listeners and starts reading the next part to them. Right after saying, "those who practice such things deserve to die," he launches into a shocking tirade that begins with, "How DARE you judge them!" So it was meant to be a bit startling, to get their attention.

As you continue to read the chapter, you'll see that in Romans 2:17 Paul's audience becomes clear: the ones who "rely on the law." This nails it—he was definitely talking to unconverted Jews. He was saying that because they had the Law and esteemed it, they assumed they were good with God. Verses 17-24 are the lynchpin. This is where the entire issue becomes crystal clear.

*But if **you call yourself a Jew** and rely on the law
and boast in God and know his will and approve what is excellent,
because you are instructed from the law;
and if you are sure that you yourself are a guide to the blind,
a light to those who are in darkness, an instructor of the foolish,
a teacher of children, having in the law the embodiment
of knowledge and truth—
you then who teach others, do you not teach yourself?
While you preach against stealing, do you steal?
You who say that one must not commit adultery,
do you commit adultery?
You who abhor idols, do you rob temples?
You who boast in the law, you dishonor God by breaking the law.
For, as it is written,
"The name of God is blasphemed among the Gentiles
because of you."*

After reading this, you can see why Paul would say something like, "How dare you judge them."

The two distinct groups

So here's the contrast; here are the two groups:

<u>Romans 1</u>: Those *heathen pagan Gentiles* who wanted to break laws, flagrant in their sin, even if they knew it would lead to death.

<u>Romans 2</u>: The *religious Jews* who had the Law and "kept" the Law and taught others to "keep" the Law, and even taught little children, and yet were breaking the Law in at least some of the same ways as the Gentiles, but doing it in secret.

The "you" of Romans 2:1 applies to you *only if you're in the category being described in Romans 2:17-24.*

Who are those people today?

It would be a perversion of everything the Word of God says about the new life of Christ in the believer to say that this Scripture applies to all Christians, the ones whose hearts are made new in Jesus Christ.

But there are people who fit in this category. At the same time that they're loudly and proudly proclaiming, "We are the holy people," at the same time that they may be condemning some other group of people (according to race or belief system or political affiliation or whatever), they're secretly breaking laws they purport to keep.

I know some people struggle with an interpretation of Scripture like this. That is, an interpretation that lays the blame for wickedness right squarely at the feet of the wicked and does NOT say that a heart-renewed child of God who sins by being impatient with your child (or something similar) is analogous to the *massive evil of malignant narcissistic, sociopathic, sadistic abuse* you described your friend as having endured.

So I hope there won't be any sense of false guilt in understanding the truth of what God is saying here. I hope instead there will be freedom.

How to pray

Regarding how to pray for judgment against the wicked, I believe it's appropriate and Biblical and Kingdom-oriented to pray for swift judgment "according to His will" on those who execute and enable wickedness. Our Lord may in fact turn some hearts to Himself, as He did with the apostle Paul, who did what he did "ignorantly in unbelief."[2] We trust Him to accomplish what is right

---

[2] 1 Timothy 1:13.

in the lives of those who scorn His truth and righteousness, His holiness and love.

I'm praying that the church of Jesus Christ will awaken and will uproot these roots of bitterness in their midst. But we can understand our world and our God far better when we understand how to read passages like this one and see to whom the Scriptures apply. I hope this helps.

Love,
Rebecca

UNTWISTED TRUTH FROM CHAPTER 5

- ❖ It's important to apply the Rule of Pronouns to Scripture when we read it. (Who was it originally written to? Do I also fit in that category?)
- ❖ The indictment of Romans 2 must be taken in the greater context of the entire book of Romans.
- ❖ There are those who fit the category of the Romans 2 lawbreakers, but it is not "all Christians." It is those who claim to be the people of God while simultaneously secretly living in heart mutiny against Him.

CHAPTER 6

Why "I'm the Worst Sinner I Know" Is Unbiblical

The teaching

You may have been taught that each Christian is supposed to think "I'm the worst sinner I know." It may even be ingrained in your thinking. It may feel like an unhealthy way to think, but the more important question is, is it a *Scriptural* way to think?

It can be confusing, if you've lived in an abusive environment and if you've been taught to read the Scriptures a certain way.

When C.J. Mahaney, the founder of Sovereign Grace Ministries (SGM) began proclaiming "I'm the worst sinner I know" somewhere around the late 1990s, it certainly wasn't the first time this teaching had been promoted.[1] But from what I could find, this was when it began to go mainstream.

Mahaney himself claimed it regularly, often even as a way of introducing himself when he would stand up to speak. "I'm C.J.

---

[1] When I traced the modern resurgence of that statement, I found that it actually originated in 1994 in Gary Thomas's book *Seeking the Face of God*. (This is the same Gary Thomas who told people marriage was supposed to make them holy rather than happy, which appeared to condone abuse.) *Seeking the Face of God* is out of print, but it was republished in 2011 with a new title, *Thirsting after God*.

Mahaney, and I'm the worst sinner I know." But it isn't only Mahaney who is supposed to be the worst sinner he knows. Each one of us is supposed to be the worst sinner each one of us knows. In 2002 Mahaney wrote in *The Cross-Centered Life: Keeping the Gospel the Main Thing*:

> Every one of us can honestly claim that "worst of sinners" title. No, it isn't specially reserved for the Adolf Hitlers, Timothy McVeighs, and Osama bin Ladens of the world. William Law [a 17th-century writer] writes, "We may justly condemn ourselves as the greatest sinners we know because we know more of the folly of our own heart than we do of other people's." . . . So admit you're the worst sinner you know.[2]

This appears to be when the teaching caught hold and spread way beyond Mahaney's Sovereign Grace Ministries circles.

In 2008 at one of the many huge conferences he frequented, Mahaney gave an interview about being the worst sinner he knows.

> Oh, I do indeed [believe I'm the worst sinner I know]. Yeah. And here's why I believe that. Because I'm more familiar with my sins than I am with anyone else's sins. When I stay close to the doctrine of sin and apply the doctrine of sin, in the shadow of the cross, to my soul, I am indeed the worst sinner I know, in light of God's holiness, my sinfulness as I consider my heart, yes, I am convinced. Now, when I drift from that, and when I evaluate other people and compare myself favorably with someone then no, I become arrogant, I become self-righteous. . . .[3]

---

[2] C.J. Mahaney, *The Cross-Centered Life: Keeping the Gospel the Main Thing*, Crown Publishing Group, 2002, p 44.

[3] Q&A with James MacDonald, from the Straight Up Conference in Elgin IL, uploaded by Sovereign Grace Churches, October 7, 2008. https://vimeo.com/5461878.

CHAPTER 6 – WHY "I'M THE WORST SINNER I KNOW" IS UNBIBLICAL

Interviewer: So you really mean positionally and potentially and by terms of the darkness of which I am capable, I am the worst sinner I know. You don't mean practically, as I'm living my life today, if we could bring forward a sampling of twenty people in the church and read off our failures of the last thirty days, I would be the most sinful person on that list.

Mahaney: No, I would say I would, but here's why. Because I'm familiar with my sin.

Interviewer: But in a moment we're going to be familiar with everyone's, cause we're all going to read our list.

> Mahaney: Uh, yeah, even, even when the list was read, I would, I would, I think I would still argue that, uh, your list, though serious, uh, is, is different from what I'm familiar with in my own soul as I contemplate manifestations of pride and lust and anger and complaining, uh, desire to impress, just all the forces that war against my soul on a daily basis, uh, some of which I commit on a daily basis. I'm intimately familiar with them in a way I'm not with yours, regardless of what you confess.[4]

Interviewer: You don't feel the horror about my sin that you feel about your own.

Mahaney: I don't. I don't.

Interviewer: That's clear. I think you've given us a lot to think about.

Mahaney: Yeah. In terms of familiarity, I'm more familiar with mine than yours. I know mine up close and personal.

Interviewer: I think that's very helpful. It gives us . . . I gotta think about that. That's fantastically clear, and I really appreciate it.[5]

Somehow Mahaney wanted to equate being familiar with one's own sins to thinking that one's sins were the worst.

---

[4] Ibid.
[5] Ibid.

Even while he was saying it was "fantastically clear," the interviewer sounded puzzled. I was puzzled too. I got the impression that the interviewer—being a friend of Mahaney's and all—saw that he was causing Mahaney to stutter and stammer in his reply and needed to back off to keep everything comfortable. But there are problems. Big problems. But that didn't stop the teaching from becoming ubiquitous. Here are just a few examples.

> I read a quote on Twitter the other day. . . . "If the biggest sinner you know isn't you, then you don't know yourself very well." . . . If I'm honest, deep down, probably not even that deep, I don't consider myself the worst of sinners. But I can tell you, the more I learn about the righteousness of God and the more I examine my own life and motives—the closer I'm getting to the inescapable conclusion that I am the worst sinner I know.[6]

> We need to be experts at finding and rooting out our own sin—no one else's. We have plenty to deal with right here in our own heart without having to take on anyone else's sin as our personal campaign. I am the worst sinner I know simply because I know myself better than anyone. My sin is the worst because it is mine.[7]

> When people criticize me or talk about what a horrible sinner I am, my posture is to agree with them, not defend. I will be the first in line to build a case against myself, I am the worst sinner I know because I know my sin the most.[8]

---

[6] Kyle Idleman, *Grace is Greater: God's Plan to Overcome Your Past, Redeem Your Pain, and Rewrite Your Story,* Baker Publishing Group, 2017, pp 28-29.
[7] John Fischer, *12 Steps for the Recovering Pharisee (like me),* Baker Publishing, 2000, pp 100-101.
[8] Josh Weidmann, *The End of Anxiety: The Biblical Prescription for Overcoming Fear, Worry, and Panic,* Salem Books, 2020.

The untwisting

The "worst sinner" reference is from 1 Timothy 1:15-16, when Paul was speaking about the grace God had shown to him.

In the interview referenced above, Mahaney said,

> But in Paul's ability to say he was the worst sinner, the worst of sinners—yet who could be more corrective than Paul?—I think that's a combination that I want to aspire to.

Being the worst sinner AND correcting other people a lot. That was (and I assume still is) Mahaney's aspiration.

> [Paul's] focus is not primarily outward. It's inward. . . . He is saying, in effect, "Look, I know my sin. And what I've seen in my own heart is darker and more awful; it's more proud, selfish, and self-exalting; and it's more consistently and regularly in rebellion against God than anything I have glimpsed in the heart of anyone else. As far as I can see, the biggest sinner I know is me."[9]

If you study the writings of the Apostle Paul—there are many!—you'll see that these words don't describe him at all. He talked about himself all through the epistles, and nothing he said even comes close to this kind of description.

> [My seminary professor pointed out] Paul didn't say, "I *was* the worst of sinners." He said, "I *am* the worst of sinners."[10]

But I would argue that Paul never said this. Keep reading.

---

[9] Dave Harvey, *When Sinners Say I Do,* Shepherd Press, 2010, Kindle edition Loc 416-432.

[10] Kyle Idleman, *Grace is Greater,* p 28. Kyle talks about the same thing in several of his other books, such as *Grace from the Cross* (2018), and *The Grace Effect: What Happens When Our Brokenness Collides with God's Grace* (2017).

In order to come up with the interpretation that Mahaney and others have concluded, it's important to read 1 Timothy 1:15-16 in the New International Version. Here it is:

Here is a trustworthy saying that deserves full acceptance:
Christ Jesus came into the world to save sinners—
*of whom **I am the worst**. But for that very reason*
*I was shown mercy so that in me, **the worst of sinners**,*
Christ Jesus might display his immense patience as an example
for those who would believe in him and receive eternal life.

It sure does look like Paul said exactly what they claim he said.

But see where Paul said "the worst" and "the worst of sinners"? Both of those come from one Greek word, *protos*.

The NIV was published in 1984. Before that, every version of the Bible translated the word as what it means: "chief" or "foremost." Here are two of them.

The saying is trustworthy and deserving of full acceptance,
that Christ Jesus came into the world to save sinners,
*of whom I am the **foremost**. (ESV)*
This is a faithful saying, and worthy of all acceptation,
that Christ Jesus came into the world to save sinners;
*of whom I am **chief**. (KJV)*

So what does it mean? Does "foremost" or "chief" mean "worst of sinners"?

This Greek word *protos* sometimes means "first in time or space." That's obviously not the meaning here, because God showed mercy to other people before He showed mercy to Paul.

The only other meaning for the word is "of primary significance." Here are some examples of that meaning for *protos*. There are enough that I believe it will be quite convincing that in this context the word means "of primary significance." There is absolutely no basis for thinking it means "worst."

Matthew 6:33
*But seek **first** the kingdom of God and his righteousness*
[give it primary significance in your life],
and all these things will be added to you.

Matthew 20:27 (KJV)
*And whosoever will be **chief** among you [most significant],*
let him be your servant:

Matthew 22:37-38
You shall love the Lord your God with all your heart
and with all your soul and with all your mind. This is the great
*and **first** commandment [the one of primary significance].*

Luke 15:22
But the father said to his servants,
*'Bring quickly the **best** robe [literally, the protos robe,*
the one of primary significance], and put it on him. . . .

Luke 19:47b
*The **chief** priests [the ones of primary significance]*
*and the scribes and the **principal** men of the people*
were seeking to destroy him,

Acts 13:50
But the Jews incited the devout women of high standing
*and the **leading** men of the city [the ones of primary significance],*
stirred up persecution against Paul and Barnabas,
and drove them out of their district.

Romans 3:1-2 (NKJV)
What advantage then has the Jew?
or what is the profit of circumcision?
*Much in every way! **Chiefly** [primarily],*
because to them were committed the oracles of God.

There are more, but that seems sufficient to prove my point.

There is no reason in the world to translate the word *protos* in 1 Timothy 1:15 any differently. Thus, with those Scriptures as the backdrop, we can be quite certain that this is what Paul was saying in 1 Timothy 1:15:

> *The saying is trustworthy and deserving of full acceptance,*
> *that Christ Jesus came into the world to save sinners,*
> *of whom I am **of primary significance.***

Why would Paul say that? The next verse, verse 16, explains more, here in the ESV:

> *But I received mercy for this reason, that in me,*
> *as the **foremost** [there's protos again—*
> *the one of primary significance],*
> *Jesus Christ might display his perfect patience as an **example**
> *[KJV "pattern"]*
> *to those who were to believe in him for eternal life.*

But again the NIV translates verse 16 irresponsibly, using "worst of sinners" in place of the one Greek word meaning "of primary significance."

The English word *prototype* comes from the Greek word *protos*, with the Oxford English Dictionary defining it to mean, "The first or primary type of a person or thing; an original on which something is modeled or from which it is derived; an exemplar, an archetype."[11]

Paul wasn't the first person chronologically to be pulled from the depths of sinfulness to be shown the abundant grace of God. But Paul did regularly present himself as an example, an archetype, a "pattern" to the people to whom he wrote, throughout his epistles. In this, he was communicating this message:

"God showed mercy on one who was completely opposed to His great salvation, then making me no less than an apostle. This

---

[11] "prototype," n. and adj. *Oxford English Dictionary*, Clarendon Press, 1991.

gives an example (or pattern, or archetype) of the perfect patience of Jesus Christ for those who will believe on Him."

This is why he could say in 1 Corinthians 11:1, *Follow me as I follow Christ.*

Paul spoke to Timothy in the present tense not because he currently viewed himself as just as terrible a sinner as he was before his conversion, as Mahaney and others have indicated, but because he was, at the time he was speaking, a pattern-maker, an archetype.

Also, Paul spoke about himself alone—he wasn't saying anything about how other Christians were or are supposed to view themselves.[12] Paul wasn't showing a kind of humility he expected us all to follow by saying, "I'm the worst sinner I know, and you are, by logical extension, the worst sinner you know."

That wasn't his point at all. His point was to hold himself up as an example.

> *Self-deprecation is not the same as humility. Spiritualizing shame, self-hatred, self-loathing is a dangerous misappropriation that doesn't align with God's heart for us. We are not called to join heart postures or perspectives toward ourselves that He does not endorse.*[13]

The implications of this different interpretation are huge. Paul didn't live in the life of miserable failure he described in the second half of Romans 7.[14] He lived in the life of victory described in Romans 8 and in all the many other victorious Scriptures he wrote.

---

[12] Another example of an instance when Considering the Pronouns sheds light on our understanding of Scripture.

[13] Elisa Malpass, personal correspondence, June 24, 2022. Used by permission.

[14] For more on this, see "The Trump Card of Romans 7," Here's the Joy, May 20, 2021, https://heresthejoy.com/2012/05/the-trump-card-of-romans-7/

The difference between the "sinners" and the "sins"

So, are any people "worst sinners"?

Funny thing about that. In many evangelical churches, there seems to be a disparity. On the one hand, we're all supposed to believe that we're the worst sinner we know.

And on the other hand, we're supposed to believe that "sin is sin" and "all sins are equal," showing a total lack of understanding of the concept of degrees of sin.

I would say, though, that I believe the Scriptures teach the opposite. That is, if you flip these two ideas, you'll get what I believe the Bible teaches.

Both the Scriptures and life experience teach that some sins are worse than others and that if allowed to continue, sins will often progress from bad to worse. At the same time,

---

The Scriptures also teach that when the sinners themselves stand at the foot of the cross, they stand on equal ground. That is, every person is equally in need of the salvation Jesus Christ provides.

A Christian may speak of what a great sinner he was before the Lord saved him, even using the hyperbole "chief of sinners" or "worst of sinners." Also, those of us who were "good" people growing up can after our salvation come to a deeper realization or understanding of our own sin. I know this experientially because it happened to me. Though I still regularly need to turn from sin, in my adult Christian life I experienced three major episodes when I came face to face with noxious sin in my life from which I desperately needed to be delivered.

But I didn't stay in a place of considering myself so utterly overcome with sin that I was stuck in "worst sinner" quicksand. Instead, I looked to the Lord for deliverance from it. I expected deliverance. And the Lord did deliver me. He continues to do so, regularly.

Paul lived in victory, not defeat

The only way a devoted Christian like Paul would continually see himself as the "worst of sinners" would be to constantly analyze his motives, always finding them full of corruption. But even though Paul talked about himself in the epistles hundreds and hundreds of times, he never once agonized over pride or self-centeredness.

In fact, if you believe that Paul thought he was the worst sinner he knew, it might be a little unnerving to read 2 Corinthians, for example. If you pay attention, you'll see that Paul talked and talked and talked about all the good things he did, all the ways he helped the Corinthian Christians, all the concern he felt for them, all the persecution and other trials he had undergone for their sakes. And never once did he even imply that he was agonizing over his motives. In fact, he said just the opposite. For example, in 2 Corinthians 4:1-2 he said,

Therefore, having this ministry by the mercy of God,
we do not lose heart. But we have renounced disgraceful,
underhanded ways. We refuse to practice cunning
or to tamper with God's word,
but by the open statement of the truth we would commend ourselves
to everyone's conscience in the sight of God.

Here's the Amplified Classic Bible (AMPC) for verse 2.

We have renounced disgraceful ways
(secret thoughts, feelings, desires and underhandedness,
the methods and arts that men hide through shame);
we refuse to deal craftily (to practice trickery and cunning)
or to adulterate or handle dishonestly the Word of God....

Paul never talked about how he was sinning with every thought, word and deed, or claimed that all his deeds were filled with corruption, as we are so often taught.[15] Instead, he talked about how he was striving to take the gospel of the Kingdom to farther and farther places around the world and was willing to undergo deprivation in order to accomplish this goal.

I think Paul saw his life as a laser beam pointing to Jesus Christ—he wasn't flawless but focused. When his thoughts started to turn away, for example, in discouragement—which was significant in this epistle—he pointedly turned them back. The (lack of) transition from 2 Corinthians 2:13 to 2:14 is an excellent example. Starting here with verse 12:

> *When I came to Troas to preach the gospel of Christ,*
> *even though a door was opened for me in the Lord,*
> *my spirit was not at rest*
> *because I did not find my brother Titus there.*
> *So I took leave of them and went on to Macedonia.*
>
> *BUT thanks be to God,*
> *who in Christ always leads us in triumphal procession,*
> *and through us spreads the fragrance of the knowledge of him everywhere.*

So in modelling my Christian life after the prototype Paul, here's what I seek to do. If a thought starts to challenge me about my motives, saying, for example, *You know that all you really want is your own glory. Your motives are corrupt and all these efforts to please God are filthy rags. . . .*

I don't even start analyzing the thought, trying to figure out if any aspect of my motives were pure and how overwhelmingly much may be corrupt. Instead, I see this thought for the garbage it is. I actively respond, *Jesus Christ! In You alone I am perfectly*

---

[15] Ibid.

pleasing to God. You are the cleanser of my motives. You will be glorified in me, in spite of who and what I could be outside of You.

By the power of Christ, I renounce these thoughts. I refuse to accept them. I turn to Jesus, as He tells us through 2 Corinthians 10:5, taking "every thought captive to obey Christ."

The understanding of this spiritual activity within, which Paul shows so clearly in 2 Corinthians (as well as other epistles), was a big part of what could keep him focused and full of energy—we can even say full of love and hope—in the face of one discouragement after another.

It seems perfectly clear to me that Paul didn't obsess over his motives. He didn't have time to pay a lot of attention to them. He was looking at Jesus.

I pray we can all do the same.

UNTWISTED TRUTH FROM CHAPTER 6

- ❖ The Greek word *protos* in 1 Timothy 1:15-16 doesn't mean "worst of sinners." It means "chief" or "foremost," "one of primary significance."
- ❖ Paul's epistles bear witness that though he talked about himself often, he did not obsess over his motives.
- ❖ Though all sins are not equal, all sinners are equally in need of saving.
- ❖ Paul did not see himself as the worst of sinners, but as an ambassador for Jesus Christ, consistently victorious.
- ❖ Paul saw himself as a "prototype," an example for other believers.
- ❖ We can all follow Paul's example.

CHAPTER 7

How Teaching Christians to Embrace "I'm the Worst Sinner I Know" Harms the Body of Christ

So, you might say, "I'm the worst sinner I know" may not have any Biblical basis. But is it really harmful? Isn't it a useful tool to help us all be more humble?

No.

Generally, false teachings are not useful in the body of Christ.

The environment created by this teaching

It's hard to understand how a God-fearing, Jesus-loving Christ-follower could live in a constant state of being as terrible a sinner as C.J. Mahaney described, referenced in the preceding chapter, unless his fight against sin is a complete failure.

This thought leads to some serious implications about the (lack of) power of the Holy Spirit.

When Christians apply "I'm the worst sinner I know" to themselves, we'll find it to be a severe liability rather than a help in the body of Christ in three primary ways:

> It will keep earnest Christians in a constant state of introspection, which can lead to depression and despair.
> Ironically, it can be used to exalt leaders.
> It will keep Christians from pointing out serious and even dangerous sins in others.

Here is how I believe each one of these can result from this false teaching.

"I'm the worst sinner I know" can lead to depression and despair rather than living in the victory and joy Christ promises

In the same interview cited in chapter 6, the interviewer asked,

> *But practically, if I'm the worst sinner I know, in what sense am I not unqualified to teach and minister to people? If I am in practice the worst sinner in my church?*[1]

Mahaney replied,

> Well, if you weren't opposing your sin, if you weren't, as Ryle said, quarreling with your sin, fighting your sin, by God's grace subduing your sin, growing in godliness, then you wouldn't be qualified.[2]

The "worst sinner I know" teaching emphasizes seeking out your sin so you can, as Mahaney says, "oppose it," "quarrel with it," "fight it," and "subdue it." This is apparently the way you are supposed to "grow in godliness."

None of which the Bible says to do. In fact, the Scriptures say in Romans 6 that we have been set free from sin.[3]

---

[1] Q&A with James MacDonald, from the Straight Up Conference in Elgin IL, uploaded by Sovereign Grace Churches, October 7, 2008. https://vimeo.com/5461878.

[2] Ibid.

[3] More on this in chapter 15.

The Scriptures tell us to seek many things, so many, in fact, that I did a subject study on that once years ago.[4] Our sin is never named as one of the things we should seek. The primary focus of our hearts and our eyes is to be upward to the Lord, not inward to our sin.

If it's followed fully and wholeheartedly, this mentality of "you'll always be the worst sinner you know, but you need to keep fighting your sin anyway" will lead to Despair. Like Sisyphus of ancient Greek mythology, the Christian is apparently to keep laboring away at a task which he is notified ahead of time will always miserably fail.

According to these teachers, when we present the gospel to anyone, what are we offering? Not release from sin. Rather, more guilt than they've ever experienced, lasting guilt from which they can never escape. I've spoken with several people who have struggled under such a burden.

Is this good news?

If we tell people they must believe they're the worst sinner they know and will never be able to escape this condemnation, then we're negating the truth of Romans 8:1,

> *There is therefore now **no condemnation** for those who are in Christ Jesus.*

"I'm the worst sinner I know" can be used as a weapon against others for self-exaltation and manipulation

Mahaney declared on Twitter, "I become self-righteous when I do not consider myself the worst sinner I know." When a person states unequivocally that he is the worst sinner he knows, then, we assume, he must not be self-righteous or proud, right? It seems

---

[4] Just in the New Testament, we are told to seek those things which are above (Colossians 3:1-2), the kingdom of God (Matthew 6:33), honor from God (John 5:44), the building up of others (1 Corinthians 10:24), and the Lord Himself (Hebrews 11:6).

impossible for the two to go together. So by stating it, Mahaney was showing himself to be humble, right?

And by simply disagreeing with it, I must be showing myself to be self-righteous. You see how that works? (But because this statement is unbiblical and has been used to oppress people, I press on.)

In the interview cited above, Mahaney said:

> I think that an Edwards or those with responsibility to draw attention to sin, I think it's important for them to be walking in some degree of humility for that prophetic call to be effective. If they aren't convinced they are the worst sinner they know, then their call to repentance will be motivated to some degree by self-righteousness, I think discerned by those who are receiving it.[5]

And also . . .

> But in Paul's ability to say he was the worst sinner, the worst of sinners—yet who could be more corrective than Paul?—I think that's a combination that I want to aspire to. And I want to be careful about correcting anybody if I'm not convinced that I'm the worst sinner I know, because I don't think my correction will be humble, and it will be more difficult for them to receive.[6]

So if C.J. Mahaney says he's the worst sinner he knows, then how can you *not* receive his correction, any correction at all, in fact?

But as it turns out, it seems that Mahaney believed that he himself didn't need any correction. Maybe it was because he already thought of himself as the worst sinner he knew, so he was all set, thank you very much.

---

[5] Q&A with James MacDonald.

[6] Ibid.

In 2005, three years after *The Cross-Centered Life*, Mahaney wrote a book on humility[7] which became very popular. As a result, many non-insiders were stunned when in 2011 a former Sovereign Grace Ministries leader began to expose the truth: that for years before the publication of this book, Sovereign Grace Ministries (SGM) leaders had been formally confronting Mahaney for his pride.[8]

As one of them observed, "To correct C.J., or to challenge his own self-perception, was to experience a reaction through e-mails, consistent disagreement (without seeking to sufficiently understand), a lack of sufficient follow-up, and occasionally, relational withdrawal."[9]

In spite of his Uriah-Heep-ish 'umble talk, it appears that Mahaney considered himself above correction, effecting a high-handed leadership style and refusing to receive criticism.[10]

What eventually came out was that during the years he was tweeting and preaching that he was the worst sinner he knew, Mahaney was also apparently covering crimes,[11] participated in setting up a hush fund,[12] and even blackmailing.[13] He said he would look forward to speaking freely about a civil suit in which

---

[7] C. J. Mahaney, *Humility: True Greatness*, Multnomah Books, 2005.

[8] Brent Detwiler, "It's About Ethics, Not Polity, Stupid!" *BrentDetwiler.com*, August 24, 2012. http://www.brentdetwiler.com/brentdetwilercom/its-about-ethics-not-polity-stupid.html

[9] Dave Harvey quoted in Brent Detwiler, "A Cross Centered or Gospel Centered Legacy," *BrentDetwiler.com*, March 19, 2013. http://www.brentdetwiler.com/brentdetwilercom/a-cross-centered-or-gospel-centered-legacy.html

[10] Kris, "How SGM Leaders Actually Handle Criticism," *SGMSurvivors*, March 28, 2011. https://www.sgmsurvivors.com/2011/03/28/how-sgm-leaders-actually-handle-criticism/

[11] Todd Wilhelm, "Mahaney Has No Clothes!" *Thou Art the Man*, May 14, 2014. https://thouarttheman.org/2014/05/14/mahaney-has-no-clothes/

[12] Brent Detwiler, "Hush Fund Set Up by Top SGM Leaders to Meet the Demands of a SGM Pastor Whose Son Was Sexually Abused," *BrentDetwiler.com*, March 30, 2015. http://abrentdetwiler.squarespace.com/brentdetwilercom/hush-fund-set-up-by-top-sgm-leaders-to-meet-the-demands-of-a.html

[13] Brent Detwiler, "Open Letter Upon Release of SGM Panel Report on Tomczak Departure – 7 Concerns by Larry & Doris Tomczak," *BrentDetwiler.com*, February 1, 2012. http://www.brentdetwiler.com/brentdetwilercom/2012/2/1/open-letter-upon-release-of-sgm-panel-report-on-tomczak-depa.html

he was charged,[14] but when the suit was dismissed on technicalities, he never did speak about it.

Finally, after years of preaching the importance of submitting to church leadership, Mahaney himself left his own church peremptorily without following due process,[15] immediately starting another church with people who were loyal to him.[16] He then went on to speak at various places about suffering like Job.[17]

At one point when Mahaney spoke publicly about this scandal (again without giving any specifics), he said his sins were "respectable," "routine," and "common."[18]

So much for being the worst sinner he knew.

Following leaders such as Mahaney, other church leaders have slid into a similar way of thinking. Even if they preach "I am the worst sinner I know," they do not want to be challenged.

"I'm the worst sinner I know" sets up an environment for sin tolerance and covering of abuse

A former SGM member told me,

When a sheep corrects an arrogant shepherd, the shepherd is no longer the worst sinner he knows. That is often pointed out to the proud (and dumb) sheep. Put another way, "If you really saw your sin [sheep], you would never confront my sin [shepherd]."[19]

---

[14] Jeremy Weber, "C.J. Mahaney Breaks Silence on Sovereign Grace Ministries Abuse Allegations," *Christianity Today*, May 22, 2014. https://www.christianitytoday.com/news/2014/may/c-j-mahaney-breaks-silence-sovereign-grace-ministries-sgm.html

[15] Todd Wilhelm, "Mark Dever – Integrity Sold for $10K," *Thou Art the Man*, August 19, 2017. https://thouartheman.org/2017/08/19/mark-dever-integrity-sold-10k/

[16] Tiffany Stanley, "The Sex-Abuse Scandal that Devastated a Suburban Megachurch," *Washingtonian*, February 14, 2016. https://www.washingtonian.com/2016/02/14/the-sex-abuse-scandal-that-devastated-a-suburban-megachurch-sovereign-grace-ministries/

[17] For just one example, see C.J. Mahaney, "Sustained in Suffering by the Saga of Job," *T4G*, 2016. http://t4g.org/resources/*2016/04/sustained-in-suffering-by-the-saga-of-job/

[18] "C.J. Mahaney's Address at SGM Pastor's Conference 2011," *SGMNation*, December 11, 2011. https://sgmnation.wordpress.com/2011/12/11/cj-mahaneys-address-at-sgm-pastors-conference-2011/

[19] Anonymous, personal correspondence, March 18, 2017. Used by permission.

CHAPTER 7 – "I'M THE WORST SINNER I KNOW" HARMS THE BODY OF CHRIST

When a person is deemed to be "important to the ministry," his sins will be tolerated and covered, and the one who points them out will be the one accused. You can never point the finger, as Nathan did at David, saying, "Thou art the man," because, as they say, there will be three fingers pointing back at you.[20]

They will find you, with your own superlatively sinful heart, the most culpable, no matter what sin you're pointing out. According to many first-person accounts, even in the cases of sexual abuse at Mahaney's church,[21] this is exactly the way the abused were treated when they came to church leaders for redress of grievances.

> *The statement [I'm the worst sinner I know] reveals a stunning moral narcissism: an intentional subjective shortsightedness that requires a man to ignore the larger world around him and refuse a sense of proportion in the actions of other men.*[22]

A piece on *SGMSurvivors* gives an insightful analysis on how teaching "I'm the worst sinner I know" sets up an environment for abuses of the worst kind.

> *Because of SGM's belief that each of us must always be "the worst sinner that we ourselves know," we basically give up our rights to ANY victimhood, no matter how heinous the crime committed against us.*
>
> *In other words, even though what happened to [someone whose three-year-old daughter was atrociously abused by someone in the church] was absolutely horrific, SGM's foundational*

---

[20] See "Three Fingers Pointing Back at You," *Here's the Joy,* May 27, 2019. https://heresthejoy.com/2019/05/three-fingers-pointing-back-at-you/

[21] Bonnie Pritchett, "Covenant Life Church member arrested for abuse," *World,* April 7, 2016. https://wng.org/sift/covenant-life-church-member-arrested-for-abuse-1617423587. See also Dan Morse, "Covenant Life Church pastors face scrutiny over ex-church member's abuse," *Washington Post,* June 1, 2014. https://www.washingtonpost.com/local/crime/covenant-life-church-pastors-face-scrutiny-over-ex-church-members-abuse/2014/06/01/f439a376-e835-11e3-a86b-362fd5443d19_story.html

[22] John Immel, *Blight in the Vineyard: Exposing the Roots, Myths, and Emotional Torment of Spiritual Tyranny,* Presage Publishing, 2011. Kindle Locations 3015-3023.

teachings would say that [her] only legitimate "biblical" response would be to examine her own sinfulness and see herself as "the worst sinner" she knows. Her pastors would see it as their duty to direct [her] attention first of all to her own indwelling sin, her own wretchedness in God's eyes. I believe they sincerely think that this is "bringing the Gospel into" everything they do. For them, "the Gospel" is firstly and foremostly about our own sin. . . .

Now, enter the perp. Perp expresses sorrow and remorse for his sin. He truly IS the "worst sinner that he knows" [or at least presents himself as such] so such a mindset comes easily and naturally to him. In the eyes of his SGM pastors, he automatically then becomes the "more righteous" person, since his response is the only "truly biblical" response that they can find acceptable.

It gets worse if the victim stands up for himself/herself in any fashion. SGM pastors immediately see this as unforgiveness, which of course is a sin, which then makes the victim even WORSE than the remorseful (and therefore righteous) perp. . . .

To me, this helps to make sense of why, in SGMville, the victims are minimized while the perps are protected. It's because in SGMville, the only thing that is really righteous is seeing oneself as "the worst sinner one knows." If one has had a crime – particularly a heinous crime like child abuse – perpetrated against one, there is NO HONEST WAY that one can authentically and enthusiastically embrace "worst sinner" status in one's thinking. One instinctively knows that someone else's sin (in this case, one's perp's sin) is greater than one's own sin. So one naturally raises objections to embracing "worst sinner" status.

SGM pastors sense this and seem to hone in on it, interpreting standing up for oneself as a sign of pride and sin and unforgiveness.

Meanwhile, the perp is over in his corner crying his genuine [or false] tears of sorrow. Because he truly IS the "worst sinner he knows" at that moment [or at least knows how to play this game], he is more righteous, and hence more worthy of protection.[23]

This, in fact, precisely fits the definition of a spiritually abusive teaching. It keeps the oppressed in bondage, silence, and confusion.

Picture a church teaching how to live out "the gospel" by focusing on your own personal "indwelling sin" (rather than the power of the Holy Spirit, Christ in you), so that any sin, no matter what it is, is just as heinous as any other sin.

This will develop a perfect petri dish environment for breeding abusers with hardened consciences who can then take advantage of the ones with sensitive consciences.

If the accused abuser acts remorseful with claims of being the worst sinner he knows, then he will be absolved and restored, while the abused one is often marginalized and treated with suspicion for not being forgiving enough.

What I've seen

My passion to correct this defective and dangerous teaching comes partly because I see the abuses I've described here. But it also comes because I interact on a daily basis with those who have been abused by these teachings. Some of them find the real Jesus.

> *I lost my certainty of right and wrong after a pastor functionally okayed rampant sexual violence. I had opportunities to become promiscuous, but God kept me. God kept me, because I was His, and I told Him I didn't know for sure what was right and wrong anymore but would He keep me inside His will sexually until He repaired my moral compass.*[24]

---

[23] "Why Sovereign Grace Ministries Doesn't Like Victims," *SGMSurvivors,* September 2, 2011. https://www.sgmsurvivors.com/2011/09/02/why-sovereign-grace-ministries-doesnt-like-victims/

[24] Rhoda Hostetler, personal correspondence, June 25, 2022. Used by permission.

As hopeful as that testimony is, I also see people who walk away from oppressive churches and then just keep walking, all the way out of Christianity, far away from the Lord Jesus Christ, who is our good and loving Lord and the only Savior. This is at least in part because they believe that their oppressive church's teachings were from the Bible. But they are not from the Bible. How is it possible that they have become core doctrines?

The truth

On the other hand, the life that declares the same freedom from sin that the apostle Paul himself described[25]—that life will become one of greater and greater victory, with ever increasing love, discernment, hope, wisdom, and good works.

Are you a sinner or a saint? These are words defining one's core identity. If Christians are truly trying to hold both of these opposing identities at once, then there is the potential for some serious identity issues.

But the fact is that the New Testament never refers to God's people as sinners, but always as saints. If it feels too good to be true, maybe it's because it's the gospel.

We are new creations, dead to sin and alive in Christ.[26]

The teaching of the cross, with its substitutionary atonement and complete forgiveness, is vital to the believer, but incomplete. Instead of limiting the gospel message to focusing on sins and then being thankful for forgiveness, Christians can understand the transformation that is offered through the resurrected life of Christ and the power of the Holy Spirit that is theirs through Christ's resurrection, ascension, and seating.

This is a life of joy and not despair. This is a life that, with a constant reliance on the power of Christ, will relieve you of the

---

[25] More on this in chapter 15.

[26] Besides my own writings on these topics on *Here's the Joy*, I recommend "Which Jesus are you Trusting?" by Paul Ellis, *Escape to Reality*, December 12, 2012. https://escapetoreality.org/2012/12/12/which-jesus-are-you-trusting/

heavy burden of "bootstrap sanctification" for your spiritual growth. And this is a life that will strengthen you in service for your Lord Jesus, including calling out the wolves in sheep's clothing when necessary, without fear.

When God's people stand together in the resurrection power of the risen Christ, with their identity in Christ, in the power of the Holy Spirit, what will happen?

We will see an environment created where the people of God will love each other wisely and with compassion, an environment where we will be strengthened to stand together against actual evil.

This is what God has promised us in Christ. This is a life of joy even in darkness. This is Christianity.

UNTWISTED TRUTH FROM CHAPTER 7

- ❖ The "I'm the worst sinner I know" teaching will keep earnest Christians in a state of constant introspection, will exalt leaders, and will keep Christians from pointing out serious and even dangerous sins in others.

- ❖ The Bible never tells us to seek out our sin in order to "quarrel with it" or "subdue it." The Bible tells us we are free from sin.

- ❖ Saying "I'm the worst sinner I know" will not keep you humble. It can, in fact, increase pride.

- ❖ "I'm the worst sinner I know" can be used to create an environment in which abuses will thrive.

- ❖ True Christians are new creations, dead to sin and alive in Jesus Christ.

CHAPTER 8

To Those Who Say All Christians Are Hypocrites

I know it must grow wearying to many Jesus-lovers to hear of one Christian leader after another being accused of seriously disqualifying sins and even crimes. I become weary too, but not because I believe the accusations are false or nit-picky. No, I'm glad for any such truths that are coming out, and I'm glad criminals and hypocrites are being exposed.

It's the hypocrisy itself I grow weary of.

Hypocrisy: Presenting oneself one way in public, perceived as good, while living a different way in private, definitely bad.

One of these times the person in the news was Bill Hybels, evangelical golden boy and Leadership Summit guru, accused of long-term adultery as well as attempts at seduction, which arguably fall under the category of clergy sexual abuse.[1]

---

[1] Manya Brachear Pashman and Jeff Coen, "After years of inquiries, Willow Creek pastor denies misconduct allegations," *Chicago Tribune,* March 23, 2018. https://www.chicagotribune.com/news/breaking/ct-met-willow-creek-pastor-20171220-story.html For responses to this article, see Vonda Dyer, "Vonda Dyer's Statement re: Chicago Tribune and Bill Hybels," *VondaDyer.com,* April 8, 2018. https://vondadyer.weebly.com/blog/vonda-dyers-statement-re-chicago-tribune-and-bill-hybels. See also Nancy Ortberg, "Flawed Process, Wounded Women," *Nancy Ortberg,* April 12, 2018, https://web.archive.org/web/20180412153536/https://www.nancylortberg.com. Also, Betty Schmidt, "Shining the Light on the Truth," *Veritas Be Told,* April 10, 2018. https://veritasbetold.wixsite.com/website.

But sadly, this is when the sin levelers jump in. The article I'm addressing in this chapter, published by *Christian Today* (not *Christianity Today*) gives an excellent opportunity to address the topic of hypocrisy.

Some oft-repeated falsehoods

In his article, the UK writer says,

> [I]n the US, as here in the UK, someone is innocent until proven guilty.[2]

This is a highly misleading statement that I've addressed on my website in an article about the "innocent until proven guilty" question.[3] In short, a person who actually committed a crime is not innocent, not even until proven guilty. He is, in fact, guilty of the crime.

And in fact, if he really committed the crime, then even if he is found not guilty in court, he is still guilty of the crime. I hope those who are able to think logically can understand the logic of these statements.

The author of the *Christian Today* article also said, in regard to Bill Hybels:

> It is vital to remember that none of us can fully know what happened.[4]

Again, I've heard this one so often, but it's wrong. If a person committed a crime, then there is indeed the very real possibility that there are actually people who can know what happened—if

---

[2] David Baker, "Bill Hybels: Evangelical hypocrisy and lessons for us all," *Christian Today,* April 17, 2018. https://www.christiantoday.com/article/bill-hybels-evangelical-hypocrisy-and-lessons-for-us-all/128483.htm

[3] "That 'Innocent Until Proven Guilty' Question: A Response to Ryan Fullerton," *Here's the Joy,* January 5, 2018. https://heresthejoy.com/2018/01/that-old-innocent-until-proven-guilty-question/

[4] Baker, "Bill Hybels."

not "fully," at least enough—including those on whom the crime was perpetrated, witnesses to the crime, those who have reviewed evidence, and others such as therapists who have gone through months or years of trauma work with one on whom the crime was perpetrated.

Getting to the point

But those oft-repeated falsehoods aren't even the main point of the *Christian Today* article. His main point is that we are all hypocrites. Christians, that is. All of us Christians are hypocrites. Which means, of course, how dare we point a finger at someone else whose hypocrisy has come to light.

Even though the author recommends a life of constant repenting (being continually sorry for sins), he believes we will never be able to live in victory over hypocrisy.

As you may guess, I disagree.

It's vital to observe how Jesus used the word *hypocrite*, because we can learn the whole truth about hypocrisy from Him. The author references one statement of Jesus about it in Matthew 7:3-5, but there are others, very important others.

Here are some things Jesus makes clear about hypocrites:

A hypocrite lives for the praise of men rather than the praise of God

Jesus said, regarding the Pharisees, in Matthew 6:2, 5, and 16:

Thus, when you give to the needy, sound no trumpet before you,
as the hypocrites do in the synagogues and in the streets,
that they may be praised by others.
Truly, I say to you, they have received their reward. . . .
And when you pray, you must not be like the hypocrites.
For they love to stand and pray in the synagogues
and at the street corners, that they may be seen by others.
Truly, I say to you, they have received their reward. . . .

> *And when you fast, do not look gloomy like the hypocrites, for they disfigure their faces that their fasting may be seen by others. Truly, I say to you, they have received their reward.*

At no time did Jesus ever imply that His disciples were hypocrites just like the Pharisees. On the contrary, He warned them to avoid the hypocrites.[5]

If you do what you do for flattery, if you bask in flattery and even promote others by flattery, then this is a sign that you may well be a hypocrite.

But I dare to say through the ages and even now there have been and are some people working for God and His Kingdom without regard to praise of men and in fact sometimes in the face of much censure. They are not hypocrites.

A hypocrite makes a pretense of being close to God, but his heart is far from God

In Matthew 15:7-9, Jesus said to the Pharisees, the religious leaders of their day,

> *You hypocrites! Well did Isaiah prophesy of you, when he said: "This people honors me with their lips, but their heart is far from me; in vain do they worship me, teaching as doctrines the commandments of men."*

Is your core heart desire to be close to God or to be far from God? That will be one facet of what will determine whether or not you are a hypocrite.

I dare to say there are some people who want to honor God not only with their lips, but with their whole hearts. They want their hearts to be in close harmony with God. They want to truly know Him. They are not hypocrites.

---

[5] Matthew 16:6.

A hypocrite focuses on minutiae of the law and ignores what is important to God

Jesus said to the Pharisees in Matthew 23:23,

> *Woe to you, scribes and Pharisees, hypocrites!*
> *you tithe mint and dill and cumin,*
> *and have neglected the weightier matters of the law:*
> *justice and mercy and faithfulness.*
> *These you ought to have done, without neglecting the others.*

One of the most important ways to discern a hypocrite is to see how he treats the oppressed, the marginalized, the downtrodden. Will he practice justice? Will she show mercy? Will they show the faithfulness of our Lord Jesus Christ even when sitting with someone who has experienced complex trauma?

Or will they refuse to walk alongside and even refuse to be held accountable for evils perpetrated on the weakest and most vulnerable among us?[6]

> *God walked with me in my trauma in so many ways. I experienced a Jesus dream which greatly alleviated some hellish intrusive thoughts and irrational fears. Once, God instantly quieted the mental chaos after a flashback so the right step towards healing became obvious. He gave joy despite ongoing terror.*
>
> *If people only knew. If they knew.*[7]

I dare to say that there have been and are Christians whose heart's desire is for the Kingdom of Jesus Christ to be made known in justice, mercy, and truth. They are willing to walk with those who have experienced great harm, shining for them the light of Jesus Christ. They are not hypocrites.

---

[6] As an example, see Kate Shellnutt, "Southern Baptists Refused to Act on Abuse, Despite Secret List of Pastors," *Christianity Today*, May 22, 2022, https://www.christianitytoday.com/news/2022/may/southern-baptist-abuse-investigation-sbc-ec-legal-survivors.html

[7] Rhoda Hostetler, personal correspondence, June 25, 2022. Used by permission.

A hypocrite preaches and acts one way in public while committing evil in private and in secret

In Matthew 23:14, 25, and 27-28, Jesus said to the Pharisees,

> *Woe to you, scribes and Pharisees, hypocrites!*
> *For you devour widows' houses*
> *and for a pretense you make long prayers;*
> *therefore you will receive the greater condemnation.*
>
> *Woe to you, scribes and Pharisees, hypocrites!*
> *For you clean the outside of the cup and the plate,*
> *but inside they are full of greed and self-indulgence.*
>
> *Woe to you, scribes and Pharisees, hypocrites!*
> *For you are like whitewashed tombs,*
> *which outwardly appear beautiful,*
> *but within are full of dead people's bones and all uncleanness.*
> *So you also outwardly appear righteous to others,*
> *but within you are full of hypocrisy and lawlessness.*

This is arguably the essence of hypocrisy: the double life. Not just one who sins, but one who commits acts of evil on purpose, evil being defined as purposely thumbing the nose at God and/or purposely inflicting harm on others.

I have heard of tremendous harm being inflicted on the vulnerable, some of whom have spoken with me personally. And for many, this harm was inflicted by those who have been and in some cases still are respected as good Christians and even Christian leaders. But if we are all hypocrites as this *Christian Today* author put forth, then that means we are all living a double life. It means that none of us lives a life of integrity, being the same person in private and in secret that we are in public.

But I dare to say that there have been Christians through the ages who have lived lives of integrity, and there are Christians even today who are doing the same. They are living lives that are the same—loving God and loving others—in public, in private, and in secret. They are not hypocrites.

A hypocrite will not only turn people away from Jesus Christ, the only hope for salvation, but in many cases will actively work to draw them into his evil as well

Jesus said in Matthew 23:13 and 15,

> **But woe unto you, scribes and Pharisees, hypocrites!**
> *you shut the kingdom of heaven in people's faces.*
> *For you neither enter yourselves*
> *nor allow those who would enter to go in.*
> **Woe unto you, scribes and Pharisees, hypocrites!**
> *For you travel across sea and land to make a single proselyte,*
> *and when he becomes a proselyte,*
> *you make him twice as much a child of hell as yourselves.*

I can't even begin to count the number of adults I've talked with and heard about who have turned away from Jesus Christ because of the hypocrites in their lives, and I'm not talking just about small things. I'm talking about the pseudo-Christians like in Ezekiel 34 who pretend to be shepherds for the sheep but ignore and in some cases even devour the sheep.

Woe to these hypocrites! They would be better off if a millstone had been tied around their necks and they had been drowned in the sea before they led these little ones astray.[8]

What this false teaching accomplishes

The insidious nature of the "we are all hypocrites" teaching accomplishes a masking of much great evil—great, great evil—being done under the guise of Christianity. The allegations against Bill

---

[8] Matthew 18:6.

Hybels, which were compelling, were small compared to the great covering of evil we've seen among some church leaders.[9]

There is only one group of people that our Lord Jesus called "whited sepulchers," perhaps one of the most extreme metaphors for hypocrisy ever developed. It was to those who fit the descriptions above.

I dare to say there are those in Christendom today who truly want to see evil cast out of the churches of Jesus Christ. We must continue to discern the importance of recognizing and rejecting sin leveling.

I dare to say that there are some who are zealous for the Kingdom of God . . .

who are not living for the praise of men, not receiving or dispensing flattery . . .

who long to be close to God and live for God . . .

who truly want to focus on justice, mercy, and truth, the things that are important to God . . .

who live lives of integrity, the same in private and in secret as they are in public . . .

who will draw others to good, to the real Jesus, rather than turning them away or even drawing them into their secret evil.

Of course writers and speakers who declare that we are all hypocrites are acknowledging that they themselves are hypocrites, or at least see themselves that way.

But they are also saying that the power of God is not enough to deliver us from hypocrisy, but is impotent in this regard in our Christian lives.

And even more—and how I hope Christians who love Jesus will grasp this—they are wittingly or unwittingly covering for great evil in our churches.

---

[9] For example, see Russell Moore, "This is the Southern Baptist Apocalypse," *Christianity Today*, May 22, 2022, https://www.christianitytoday.com/ct/2022/may-web-only/southern-baptist-abuse-apocalypse-russell-moore.html

May those of us who truly love Jesus and want to see His kingdom come, those of us who are living lives of integrity, passionate for Him, lives that are the same in private and in secret as they are in public, decry this sin leveling that ultimately debilitates and undermines the church of Jesus Christ.

May we stand against a hypocrisy that declares that we are all hypocrites.

UNTWISTED TRUTH FROM CHAPTER 8

- ❖ A hypocrite lives for the praise of men rather than the praise of God. There are Christians who do not do this.
- ❖ A hypocrite makes a pretense of being close to God, but his heart is far from God. There are believers who love God with genuine love.
- ❖ A hypocrite focuses on minutiae of the law and ignores what is important to God. There are Christians who want to focus on what is important to God.
- ❖ A hypocrite preaches and acts one way in public while committing evil in private and in secret. There are Christians who live lives of integrity.
- ❖ Preaching "we are all hypocrites" makes a mockery of the power of God to help His people live lives of integrity.
- ❖ Preaching "we are all hypocrites" allows evil to thrive in our churches.

CHAPTER 9

About That "Log in Your Own Eye"

Self-examination and other-examination

Chapter 7 of this book describes how that continued self-focus regarding sin issues can become unhealthy, leading to depression, despair, and self-condemnation, as well as excusing egregious sin in others, even inadvertently. It's right and proper and Christlike to focus some attention on the thinking and mindset of how abusers work, even one's very own specific abuser.

And this brings us to this Scripture. Because for some, what I just said seems to go against what Jesus said. So let's look at it.

The "log in your eye" teaching of Jesus

In Matthew 7:3-5, Jesus said to His listeners,

> *Why do you see the speck that is in your brother's eye,*
> *but do not notice the log that is in your own eye?*
> *Or how can you say to your brother,*
> *"Let me take the speck out of your eye,"*
> *When there is the log in your own eye?*
> *You hypocrite, first take the log out of your own eye,*
> *and then you will see clearly to take the speck*
> *out of your brother's eye.*

One of the observations I made in chapter 6 was that even though all *sinners* stand as equals at the foot of the cross, *sins* are not all equivalent. This is clear from Jesus' words here. Some sins are a speck, and some are a log.

But . . . it sounds like you're always the one with the log, and the other person is always the one with the speck.

That's how this Scripture is used against those who have been violated. In essence, how dare you bring an accusation against anyone or talk about anyone else's sins. You should look at the much greater sins in your own life. Some go so far as to assume that even if Christians beg God to help them remove their "log," it will continue to be there.

> *I was told for a very long time, by many fellow Christians, that all sin is equal and my "sin in the marriage" was no different from his and I was ALWAYS told to remove the proverbial plank from my own eye and never worry about the speck in his eye. And it worked for all that time because my manipulator knew/knows that all I ever wanted to do was please God.*[1]

Even after a person is out of the direct abuse, the mindset of self-focus to self-condemnation can effectively keep her crushed and unable even to understand what it was she was dealing with.

But when Jesus spoke that "you" in Matthew 7, was that referring to everyone who heard it? And more important, does it refer to everyone who reads it now? As chapter 5 of this book explains, we can step back from that pronoun and look at who it applied to. Jesus made it clear, right there in the passage. He was speaking to "hypocrites."

Is that you? Are you a hypocrite? Well, chapter 8 of this book uses the words of Jesus to lay out what and who a hypocrite is. If the shoe fits, put it on.

---

[1] Comment by Julie on "Three Fingers Pointing Back at You," *Here's the Joy*, May 27, 2019. https://heresthejoy.com/2019/05/three-fingers-pointing-back-at-you/#comment-200077

Albert Barnes, commenting on this Scripture, wrote,

> *By first amending our own faults, or casting the beam out of our eye, we can consistently advance to correct the faults of others. There will then be no hypocrisy in our conduct. We shall also "see clearly" to do it.*[2]

He assumed that Jesus was teaching that we can be free from the log (or beam).

> *The beam, the thing that obscured our sight, will be removed, and we shall more clearly discern the "small" object that obscures the sight of our brother. . . .This qualifies us for judging, makes us candid and consistent, and enables us to see things as they are and to make proper allowances for frailty and imperfection.*[3]

To be clear, God hates hypocrisy. But this doesn't mean that you always have to live under the constant frown of God because you are doomed forever to be the one with the log in your eye. If you're living a consistent life of faith and love, for the Lord Jesus Christ and others, in public, in private, and in secret, if you're listening to the Holy Spirit, applying the written Word to your life, and open to the corrections that Jesus-loving fellow believers offer—then you're taking care of those logs.

When you have dealt with any sin patterns and hypocrisy, when you are humble before the Lord, then you are in a place to speak out about the sins in the lives of others, especially those who have harmed those in their care.

Some sins are monstrosities

There's another clarification that's needed, I believe. Jesus wasn't saying that the sin of the other person is always necessarily

---

[2] Albert Barnes, commentary on Matthew 7:4-5, *Study Light,* https://www.studylight.org/commentaries/eng/bnb/matthew-7.html

[3] Ibid.

only a "speck." Another person who claims to be a Christian may in fact be committing monstrosities.

From Adam Clarke, in his commentary on Matthew 7:

A hypocrite, who professes to be what he is not (that is, professing to be a true Christian), is obliged, for the support of the character he has assumed, to imitate all the dispositions and actions of a Christian. Consequently he must reprove sin and endeavor to show an uncommon affection for the glory of God.

Sound familiar? You may have known someone like this.

Our Lord unmasks this vile pretender to saintship and shows him that his hidden hypocrisy, covered with the garb of external sanctity, is more abominable in the sight of God than the openly professed and practised iniquity of the profligate.[4]

Strong language, Adam Clarke! Are you sure you aren't self-righteous? (I kid.)

In Acts 2 Peter preached to the Jewish leaders about how they had killed their Messiah and needed to turn to God. He didn't stay quiet because of some log in his own eye. In Acts 17 Paul preached to the Athenians about their need to know "the unknown God." He didn't let concern about a log in his eye stop him.

In 2 Samuel 12, the prophet Nathan pointed his finger at the adulterous king and said, "Thou art the man!" He didn't agonize over logs before obeying God's command to confront.

James had some scathing words in his epistle, written directly to the wealthy. What about the log in your eye, James, hmmm?

Have you noticed that when David was running from King Saul, he didn't count himself as one of the wicked? He counted himself among "the righteous," whom he described in a number of his writings such as Psalm 1:6, Psalm 5:12, and Psalm 26:1, and many others. Apparently David wasn't too worried about logs in

---

[4] Adam Clarke, commentary on Matthew 7:4-5, *Bible Hub,* https://biblehub.com/commentaries/clarke/matthew/7.htm

his eye or even those "three fingers pointed back at him" when he described the wicked.

What if Christians through the centuries had stayed quiet about abuses because they were tied up in knots about the log in their own eye? In chapter 6 of my first *Untwisting Scriptures* book I spoke about many of those Christians, the ones who "took up offenses" for others.[5] William Wilberforce who spoke up against the wealthy slaveholders of England. Amy Carmichael, who spoke up against the sexual abuse going on in Hindu temples. E.C. Bridgman about the wicked English merchants who were getting the Chinese hooked on opium in order to exploit them. And more and more and more, down through the centuries.

Brave, bold, godly, righteous people who didn't worry about logs in their eyes. This was because they understood the definition of hypocrite, and they knew that they themselves didn't fit the definition. They understood that unjust and sinful treatment of others needed to be addressed.

If they had had logs in their eyes, they had already asked the Lord to reveal them and had gotten them out. After all, Jesus indicated it's possible to do that. Not just for them, but for all of us.

A righteous change from self-examination

In his book *How He Gets into Her Head: The Mind of the Male Intimate Abuser*, author Don Hennessy says,

> The focus of our work with a client is to explore with her the reasons for and the effects of relationship abuse and violence. This is best achieved by drawing her attention to the thinking and the mindset of her abuser. This changes the focus of the woman's analysis away from self-examination. This focus of self-

---

[5] *Untwisting Scriptures that were used to tie you up, gag you, and tangle your mind,* Justice Keepers Publishing, 2016.

examination has been instigated and orchestrated by the offender right from the beginning of the relationship.[6]

But isn't self-examination Scriptural? Isn't it appropriate to look at our own sin?

I believe it's so crucial to be humbly open to the Holy Spirit's words about any way we've turned away from God, through a nudging of the Spirit or through a word from a fellow believer, that our "coming to our senses" should be ongoing all the time.[7] But this is quite different from the focus of self-examination to try to find that everlasting log, especially when you're in relationship with a Pharisaical abuser.

The former can be a joyful undertaking ("I'm turning back to You, Lord") while the latter is almost invariably agonizing and excruciating. The latter also involves a myriad of twisted teachings.

Cindy Burrell, who has a ministry to abused women at www.hurtbylove.com, wrote,

> *Sadly, the principle of logs and splinters is generally applied from an expectation of perfection, whereby we are told that we may not identify the legitimate harm another is causing until we ourselves are virtually perfect [sinless]. That is ridiculous. We are called to judge rightly, to walk in truth and righteousness AND to acknowledge hypocrisy and legitimate harm where it exists, to identify the wolves among us and remove them. I cringe to consider how many have suffered because so many believers are afraid of appearing judgmental.*[8]

According to the example of Jesus, as well as David and others, it's appropriate to focus attention on the thinking and mindset of

---

[6] Don Hennessy, *How He Gets Into Her Head: The Mind of the Male Intimate Abuser*, Attic Press, 2012.

[7] More about this in chapter 14.

[8] Cindy Burrell, comment on "Do You Always Have a Log in Your Own Eye?" *Here's the Joy*, October 7, 2020. https://heresthejoy.com/2020/10/do-you-always-have-a-log-in-your-own-eye/#comment-203529

abusers, "the wicked," as they're called in the Scriptures. David spent quite a bit of time thinking about them and describing them, in Scriptures such as Psalm 7, Psalm 27, Psalm 31, Psalm 34, Psalm 37, Psalm 109, and many others.

Here's the joy for the people of God. In Jesus Christ it's possible to stand in a readiness to turn back to Him constantly, many times a day, and still be able to call out the wicked, the "roots of bitterness" in our churches and say, "These are the ones who must be removed from the church of Jesus Christ."

We can get the logs out of our eyes. We can proceed to move forward for the Kingdom. It is not hypocritical for us to do so. In fact, it's one of the best ways we can serve the cause of Christ.

UNTWISTED TRUTH FROM CHAPTER 9

- ❖ The "you" in Matthew 7:3-5 does not refer to every person or even every Christian.

- ❖ It is possible to "remove the log" from our own eye and keep it out.

- ❖ The other person's sin isn't always a "speck." It may be a monstrosity.

- ❖ There is a difference between turning back to God when we've turned away and the excruciatingly agonizing introspection of constantly trying to find logs in our eyes.

- ❖ Many righteous people in the Scriptures weren't afraid to call out sins in others. The same is true for many righteous throughout history.

- ❖ It can be a righteous undertaking to call out the "roots of bitterness" in our midst.[9]

---

[9] For more on this, see *Untwisting Scriptures that were used to tie you up, gag you, and tangle your mind, Justice Keepers Publishing,* 2016, pp 73-96.

PART THREE

We Can Be Wise About Wickedness, Wolves, and Hypocrisy

CHAPTER 10

Making Sense of the Church's Epidemic of Abuse

There weren't any wicked people in my part of the world

Around 25 or 30 years ago when I was reading through the book of Psalms, I sighed and said to myself, "There sure are a lot of psalms about the wicked. But I don't personally know any wicked people, so these psalms seem like they don't apply to me."

Yes, it's true. That's what I said.

Then I thought, "But people in other times and in other places who have suffered persecution have had to deal with wicked people, and I know these psalms must have been a comfort to them."

And then, believe it or not, my thoughts went one step further. I thought to myself, "Maybe someday I'll know some wicked people, and then I'll be thankful for these psalms."

This is true. I really did say that.

When I read the book of Psalms these days, I remember those words. Things have changed. Now I'm thankful to have those psalms in front of me, because now I know about a lot of wicked people, through the accounts of those they've harmed.

I'm reminded of a time in my 20s when I was fervently praying for revival. I remember being so sure at that time that the problem in the church was apathy. If only people in the church, people who claimed to be Christians, wouldn't be so apathetic, but would purposely awaken to the love and glory of God . . .

Nowadays, though, I'm convinced that the primary problem in the church is not apathy. It's downright wickedness.

I need to make sense of things

In 2006 I first stepped into the world of domestic abuse in the church, green as a gourd, not even having a working familiarity with terms such as "abuse" or "PTSD." But as I listened and listened, some things still made a lot of sense.

It made sense to me that my friend's thoughts would be scattered. I thought to myself, "Well, if I'd been through what she went through for 25 years, my thoughts would be scattered too."

It didn't make sense to me at first when she told me something happened at 5:30 but then corrected herself to say it happened at 5:27. I told her anyone would say 5:30 was good enough.

Well, I got a lesson that day, that an abuser would *not* say 5:30 was fine but would accuse her of lying for saying 5:30 when it was really 5:27. Then it made sense to me that she worked to be precise to the tiniest detail in every account she gave about anything.

It made sense that she took a lot of notes in the meetings that I attended with her with the Christian counselor, even though the counselor seemed to think it was somewhat eccentric. I knew by then that her words had been twisted, and that her abuser had denied saying things he had in fact said. So it made sense that she would feel the need to have that record.

In 2012, when I began to learn about sexual abuse in the church, I embarked on an even steeper learning curve. I didn't understand why sexual abuse from the long ago past caused certain shocking responses in the present that I later learned were trauma responses. But I studied diligently in an effort to understand phenomena such as flashbacks, nightmares, and dissociation. I attended conferences and listened to seminars and online lectures. I read many books. I listened, listened, and listened some more to the abuse survivors themselves. Over time, as I began to learn how the brain worked, the phenomena I saw made more and more sense.

But when it came to facing off with great wickedness, especially in the church, no "sensible reasoning" could help me wrap my mind around the stories I was hearing from the survivors. . . .

The woman who was violently raped by a celebrity pastor who laughed at her because no one would believe her.

The veritable concentration camp being run by a patriarchal church elder at his farm.

The woman who had been completely broken into dissociative parts through violent abuse, who was used in the trafficking operation of a Christian boarding school.

And more, so much more. Child pornography, child trafficking, tremendous perversity, all perpetrated by those who appeared to be among the upstanding members of church and community.

These were the kinds of stories I began hearing from the victims or eyewitnesses sometime around 2012, and they have continued on through the years, unabated. Stories of tremendous wickedness, even literal satanic wickedness within the body of Christ. I've cried out to God again and again to enlarge my capacity to hold the hard stories of others, so that these survivors can know that someone will actually listen and care.

(*But surely, Rebecca,* you say, *surely this is just a small minority. Surely these are one-in-a-million stories.* Maybe. Even if they were, still they should be cared for. But as you listen to the tiny minority of brave ones who are willing to speak publicly, and when you become one who is willing to bear compassionate witness, you may well come to realize that it's an epidemic.)

In this particular battle of "reasoning," I was laid flat. Over time as my mind began to recover from the secondary trauma, I saw three things in particular that did not make sense.

One of those things was what is commonly called *man's inhumanity to man.* I was hearing first-hand, from the survivors themselves, about acts of such utter degradation or even torture that I didn't understand how the human mind could even devise such acts. And yet . . . according to the women and sometimes men who spoke to me, they were being done by the deacon, the choir member, the Sunday school teacher, the homeschooling father, the pastor husband, the college professor. . . .

Of course, well, yes, of course I knew about the Nazis. Of course I knew about the North Koreans. Goodness, I knew history and could tell you that the Assyrians killed people by skinning them alive.

But that was there. That was then. That was "them."

This was here. This was now. And this was "us."

I couldn't wrap my mind around it. I was laid flat.

And how was it that Christians could be so complacent, so uninterested? How could church leaders turn away? How was it that Christa Brown,[1] one example of many, tried for so many years to stop Baptist predators, but the Southern Baptist leaders treated her like an annoying gnat they needed to wave away? How could that be? How could church leaders mock—not just ignore but actually *mock*—those who had been sexually abused as children, all while keeping track of the perpetrators?[2]

I was absolutely sick. It didn't make sense.

And why wasn't God intervening? Why wasn't He changing this? Why wasn't He stopping the abuse, calling predators to account, calling the church to wake up, calling more and more people to be willing to suffer the secondary trauma of entering this world, to walk with the abused and to fight the abuse? Where was He?

Even though I was regularly being laid flat, I could see that my mind was still working to try to make sense of these things. From

---

[1] Christa Brown, *This Little Light: Beyond a Baptist Preacher Predator and His Gang*, Foremost Press, 2009.

[2] Russell Moore, "This Is the Southern Baptist Apocalypse," *Christianity Today*, May 22, 2022, https://www.christianitytoday.com/ct/2022/may-web-only/southern-baptist-abuse-apocalypse-russell-moore.html

the beginning, in 2012, I mentally made categories that overlapped like Venn diagrams.[3]

Making sense

So my "making sense" of #1 (man's inhumanity to man) came in the form of understanding that yes, monstrous evil had invaded and infested the churches and sometimes had even set up churches, *because what better way to hide monstrous evil than behind a church?*

To fully grasp this whole picture took me several years, much prayer and Scripture, listening to abuse survivors, reading and listening to those who began understanding these issues decades before I did, and sleep (because that's one way I recover from grief).

There came a time when I did finally grasp it. I've seen and heard up close, from the mouths of the survivors, that the human heart—I'm talking about the unregenerate human heart, the human heart with no Holy Spirit present—has absolutely unlimited capacity for evil, even while hiding behind a mask of good and even surrounding oneself with true but naïve and gullible Christians. Because what better disguise is there for evil than an entourage of true Christians?

There is great evil. It is in our churches and other Christian organizations, even perhaps in the guise of your favorite man of God.

I understand this as a matter of spiritual warfare, because the evil is entrenched in our churches, and we cannot fight it without the armor of God and the power of the Holy Spirit.

---

[3] I wrote about these categories in the early days of my advocacy work on the BJUGrace website. "Today I prayed . . ." *BJUGrace,* December 9, 2014, http://bjugrace.com/2014/12/09/today-i-prayed/An expanded version of the development of this thinking was guest posted on Leslie Vernick's site as "The other kind of hypocrisy," a repost of which you can see on *Here's the Joy,* May 31, 2017, https://heresthejoy.com/2017/05/the-other-kind-of-hypocrisy/

Making sense of #2 (how could Christians be so complacent and uninterested?) came in part with a major *mea culpa*, because I myself had been so busy with life and other forms of ministry that I simply didn't pay attention to these things. *They were not part of my world*, I said. *I didn't know any of these people*, I said.

I could not possibly have been more wrong.

Once I started to speak, I realized it was all around me—they were all around me—and I began to feel that I, as a person who had not experienced abuse, was in the minority.

Why was I so naïve? Why did I ignore this for so long? And then when I first saw it, why did I initially allow fear of it being "too horrible" to stop me from being able to go forward?[4]

Well, I have come to my senses. I am naïve no longer, I am ignoring it no longer, and I am afraid of the "horrible" no longer. I know that outside of Christ I would have the potential for evil that is every bit as great, but the fact is, I am *not* outside of Christ. I am in Jesus Christ, and Jesus Christ is in me, renewing me. So I can say that the primary evil I fight is outside of me.[5] Armed with that understanding, I became trauma informed so I could help in practical ways as I came alongside those who were suffering in ways the Christian church as a whole needs to better understand.[6]

In regard to #3 (why wasn't God intervening?), I've seen especially through personal one-on-one work with abuse survivors that He is indeed involved in the lives of these survivors in beautiful acts of healing and sometimes even miracles.

---

[4] More about this at "Reflections on My 59th Birthday: A Warrior's Tale," *Here's the Joy*, September 5, 2016. https://heresthejoy.com/2016/09/reflections-on-my-fifty-ninth-birthday-a-tale/

[5] More about this in chapters 1, 2, 3, 14, 15, and 16 of the book you're reading now. Also, more in my book *Prayer Armor for Defense Against the Enemy's Flaming Darts*, Pennycress Publishing, 2019.

[6] On May 23, 2022, an "abuse study committee" of the Presbyterian Church of America released a report offering advice and best practices in cases of domestic abuse, sexual abuse, and spiritual abuse. Though this was only a preliminary study with only recommendations, it is one example of a denomination trying to take steps in the right direction in this regard. Read more at "PCA Abuse Study Committee Releases Its Report," by Megan Fowler, *byFaith*, May 26, 2022, https://by-faithonline.com/pca-abuse-study-committee-releases-its-report/

I am also learning more about "you have not because you ask not." What if we as His people were to be more unified in both individual and corporate prayer against the evil and for healing of the wounded and cleansing of His church, praying for the ones who have survived the unspeakable and remain silent out of fear, praying for the ones who at this very moment are being abused and tortured in ways that many Christians would find beyond the realm of imagining? What if we as His people would truly pray?

Then we would see our Lord doing even more miracles, rescuing the oppressed, healing their trauma, and revitalizing His church beyond the programs and curricula and formulas and plans.

> *Trauma does not diminish God's presence and voice. It can even amplify it, not because trauma makes us special, but because He is near to the brokenhearted who trust in Him. Our believing survivors are among our prophets, our discerners, our gifted merciful. Other believers lose so very much when shrugging off our voices as being too hypervigilant, too alarmist, too broken, too antagonistic, too "bitter." They will lose a strong theology of suffering, an orthopraxy of compassion, an awareness of God's delight in us and our delight in Him even in suffering, and they will lose the collective call to repentance for those who harm by silence or the downplaying of our voices.*[7]

And as we listen and pray, we can act. We are, after all, His hands and feet. With us He can accomplish the good work of loving and healing that He desires to do.[8]

In my own quiet way, in my one-on-one interactions with abuse survivors, I'm seeing miracles, miracles that I haven't spoken about because the individuals involved would presently

---

[7] Rhoda Hostetler, personal correspondence, June 24, 2022. Used by permission.

[8] To see one example, see Dale Ingraham and Rebecca Davis, *Tear Down This Wall of Silence: Dealing with Sexual Abuse in Our Churches,* Justice Keepers Publishing, 2017, where a meaningful Service of Lament is described in chapter 14, pages 225-230.

prefer to remain private. But it has impressed me again how very greatly the church of Jesus Christ needs to pray.

So this is my answer to #3, at least in part. We do not have because we do not ask. We need, in faith, *in faith*, brothers and sisters, in the power of the Holy Spirit, to keep asking, keep expecting,[9] keep standing against the spiritual forces of evil, keep scanning the skies. Even as we continue to speak and act in wisdom and boldness so that the light of truth will shine into the darkest corners, we will continue to trust that the Lord God, our Abba Father, our Savior Jesus Christ who loves His people, will bring justice rolling down like waters and righteousness like a mighty river.

He has not forsaken His people. He will accomplish His good work. Let us pray.

UNTWISTED TRUTH FROM CHAPTER 10

- ❖ Even the "sophisticated, cultured" areas of the world have in them those who practice great evil against others, even in the churches.

- ❖ We can ask our Lord, who has all capacity, to increase our capacity to hold the hard stories of others.

- ❖ We can become trauma informed in order to help those who are suffering the effects of trauma.

- ❖ We must continue to stand steadfast in Him against the forces of evil, through the power of the Holy Spirit, in prayer and faith.

---

[9] See "What Can We Expect from God?" *Here's the Joy,* July 20, 2022. https://heresthejoy.com/2022/07/what-can-we-expect-from-god/

CHAPTER 11

On the Proliferation of Wolves in the Churches

Someone asked me,

When the Bible talks about wolves in sheep's clothing, is that referring to a common occurrence? That in our everyday churches, there would be people there who may be well respected but are there to deceive and destroy?

Let's see about an answer here.

Riddle: How does one recognize a vicious wolf, if he looks like a harmless sheep?

So . . . I went to the Bible to see everything it has to say about wolves. Quite a bit, as it turns out.

Jesus spoke of wolves in the Sermon on the Mount

In the latter part of in His ministry, Matthew 10 and Luke 10 describe Jesus sending the Seventy out to preach the Kingdom of Heaven. He told them He was sending them out as lambs in the midst of wolves. The context indicates they were going to people who would resist the message of the Kingdom of God, sometimes violently.

That's different from finding wolves in our midst among the people of God, something Jesus warned about at the very beginning of His ministry. In Matthew 7:15 (NET) He said,

Watch out for false prophets,
who come to you in sheep's clothing
but inwardly are voracious wolves.

The difference is, in the case of the Seventy, they were going into the places where undisguised wolves would be found. In Matthew 7, Jesus described the wolves as coming into their midst, and in disguise.

In the spirit of Watching the Pronouns described in chapter 5, let's check who Jesus was speaking to. It was a group of Jews, a large crowd listening to His Sermon on the Mount. Most of these people knew very little about who Jesus was, so we won't immediately conclude for certain that this passage applies to Christians.

Jesus made it clear to His listeners that false prophets—that is, those claiming to have a word from the Lord for you—would be found among them. These were not just wolves, but *voracious* wolves.

That Greek word translated "voracious" here is also in some Scriptures translated in noun form as "extortion." *Extortion* can be defined as using one's position or power to obtain money, property, patronage, and/or greater authority and power. Hmmm.

At this very early time in His ministry, Jesus was setting the stage for His later confrontation with the religious rulers. He was already labeling them right here. By saying "Watch out," He told all His listeners to be on their guard, be on the lookout, beware.

Jesus went on to explain that these wolves would be known by their fruits (Matthew 17:15-20).[1]

---

[1] The meaning of this concept is addressed in chapters 12 and 14.

CHAPTER 11 – ON THE PROLIFERATION OF WOLVES IN THE CHURCHES

Ezekiel spoke of wolves among the rulers of Israel

Back in the Old Testament, Ezekiel had received some dire words about the leaders of the nation of Israel. Not only the dire words about the false shepherds in Ezekiel 34, but some words about vicious beasts in Ezekiel 22. Some of these are in fact the same people as those false shepherds in Ezekiel 34, the *prophets, priests, rulers* . . . and more.

It's a sad day when some words applied to leaders among the Old Testament physical people of God seem to apply altogether too closely to leaders among the modern-day church, those who are born again by His Spirit. Here are verses 25-29:

> *The conspiracy of her prophets in her midst*
> **is like a roaring lion tearing the prey;**
> *they have devoured human lives;*
> *they have taken treasure and precious things;*
> *they have made many widows in her midst.*
> *Her priests have done violence to my law*
> *and have profaned my holy things.* . . .
> *Her princes in her midst*
> **are like wolves tearing the prey,**
> *shedding blood, destroying lives to get dishonest gain.* . . .
> *The people of the land have practiced extortion*
> *and committed robbery.*
> *They have oppressed the poor and needy*
> *and have extorted from the sojourner without justice.*

What different groups of people did Ezekiel see and describe in Ezekiel 22?

The *leaders*. These were the priests, rulers, and (false) prophets, described variously as roaring lions, devourers, robbers, murderers, defilers of holy things, *wolves tearing prey,* soul destroyers, false prophets, and vain liars getting unjust gain. They even conspired with each other about these actions.

Do you believe no conspiring takes place among religious leaders today? The sad reality is that wolves tend to run in packs. When there are wolves among the "leaders" in the churches, they will tend to spend time with each other, praising and supporting one another, while ignoring or even exploiting the sheep. Yes, as Ezekiel says about the religious leaders of his day, they even conspire to do so.[2]

The *"people."* These were not the leaders (today we might say "not those in administration or on payroll"), but what some today would call the "laity." They were the ones who followed the examples of the abusive leaders. They are described as oppressors, robbers, "troublers" of the poor and needy.

The *oppressed.* These are described variously as torn prey, souls that were devoured and destroyed, widows, poor and needy, and the foreigners in their midst—those who had come from outside of physical Israel because they wanted to worship the true God. God had explicitly told the Israelites to care for these people, the foreigners, the orphans, and the widows.

And there's an unmentioned group here, I believe. The ones who were unaware of the problem, as I was, the ones I've referenced in an article as *"possums."*[3]

In that same chapter of Ezekiel, God Himself bemoaned the lack of even one *"protector"* in Israel. Ezekiel himself appeared to have been the only true prophet of that time.

There's a lot to learn from the passage in Ezekiel.

At the time of Ezekiel, the physical people group of Israel consisted of far more unbelievers than believers, so it's not surprising that in that environment, wolves would proliferate.

---

[2] For example, I know of many first-person accounts, from people who do not know each other, of having been trafficked to "big name" leaders in religious circles. See "Christians and Conspiracy Theories," *Here's the Joy,* May 12, 2020, https://heresthejoy.com/2020/05/christians-and-conspiracy-theories-a-response-to-joe-carter-at-the-gospel-coalition/

[3] See "The Other Kind of Hypocrisy," *Here's the Joy,* May 31, 2017, https://heresthejoy.com/2017/05/the-other-kind-of-hypocrisy/

But to our horror, some of us are watching these things happen again before our eyes, within the walls of the church that claims to belong to Jesus Christ and claims to be full of regenerated people of God.

How easy it has become for the wolves to walk right in and set up shop among the sheep!

Paul spoke of wolves to the Ephesians

When Paul left the Ephesian elders for the last time (Acts 20:27-32), he gave them grave warnings, to watch out for themselves and for all the flock. Surely he had Ezekiel's words in mind when he said in verse 29:

I know that after my departure,
fierce wolves will come in among you, not sparing the flock.
And from among your own selves will arise men,
speaking twisted things to draw away the disciples after them.

How could that be? How could false teachers and "fierce wolves" arise within the flock, the very flock Paul had helped to nurture? But they did.

Till the day he died, Paul fought tirelessly against the "Judaizers," those rule-makers who wanted to infiltrate the Church of Jesus Christ and take over. They wanted to force anyone who claimed the name of "Christian" to jump through their law-keeping hoops. But though he fought against them, those list-making rule-forcers eventually got in. And with them came the wolves, the ones who would use those rules to their advantage.

In his commentary on these verses, Adam Clarke referred to

Judaizing Christians who, instead of feeding the flock, would feed themselves, even to the oppression and ruin of the Church.[4]

---

[4] Adam Clarke, commentary on Acts 20:29, *Study Light,* https://www.studylight.org/commentaries/eng/acc/acts-20.html

Can you see his allusion to the "shepherds" of Ezekiel 34:2?

Ah, shepherds of Israel who have been feeding yourselves! Should not shepherds feed the sheep?

And yes, it seems like we've seen more than a few of those in the modern-day church. After studying Paul's admonition to the Ephesians, I can go back to Jesus' words to the crowd in Matthew 7:15 and think, yes, that can certainly apply to us.

What will make a church more susceptible to wolves?

Riddle: How does one recognize a vicious wolf, if he looks like a harmless sheep?

In the modern-day Western church there appear to be a few ways a church can become more susceptible to wolves, voracious wolves who tear their prey ... and, remember, it is all while looking like sheep. Here are two possibilities. You may be aware of more.

The Judaizing (that is, law-loving) wolf

Paul fought vehemently against the ones who wanted to bring the New Covenant people of God back under the law. Why was this problem so vital to him? Because they wanted to turn true Christians away from the "simplicity" that is in Christ (2 Corinthians 11:3 KJV), the sincere, unaffected gospel that I've described in several chapters of this book and in many articles on my website.

The way the Judaizers appear in the modern church is a little different from Paul's time (no more emphasis on circumcision for righteousness), but it's still a focus on the outward.

A church might as well hang a "Wolves Welcome" sign over the doorway if their focus is on "looking good" and "acting right" and "sounding right" (in public, of course)—the Christian life as a life lived by rules instead of a life lived by walking in the Holy Spirit.[5] Because then the ones who are the best at keeping the rules, whatever they may be, are the ones who make the best impression of being "good Christians." It's pretty easy to appear righteous if your righteousness is found by keeping a certain man-made list.

It's important, of course, for the private and secret life of the wolf never to be substantially questioned or investigated. In the case of elders, it's important for certain Biblical requirements of elders in Titus and 1 Timothy to be more or less ignored.[6]

The charismatic (that is, attractive and appealing) wolf

Another way a church can open itself to wolves, I believe, is by focusing on church as a business in need of business-model-type thinking, instead of as a ministry that needs faith, prayer, and the guidance of the Holy Spirit. The "human resources" focus of a church like this will be on "visionaries," strong administrators, "leaders," motivating managers, wealthy donors, compelling speakers, and good speech writers.[7]

> *Naïve, trusting believers tend to have too much trust in anyone with a "Christian" label, but they are especially susceptible to the charismatic, clever, well-spoken wolves who dress like shepherds. They don't realize they do not act anything like shepherds, because the institution cleverly rewrote the description.*[8]

A wolf can enter by this means because he or she will be appreciated (possibly even idolized) for these abilities or others.

---

[5] The Spirit will always point us to the finished work of Christ and the righteousness He gives us as we look to Him in faith.

[6] Such as being above reproach (1 Timothy 3:2 and Titus 1:6-7), being sober minded and self-controlled (1 Timothy 3:2 and Titus 1:8), not violent but gentle (1 Timothy 3:3 and Titus 1:7), not quarrelsome (1 Timothy 3:3), not arrogant or quick-tempered (Titus 1:7), a lover of good, upright and holy (Titus 1:8).

[7] See Tim Davis and Rebecca Davis, "The Business Model Church: Spiritually Bankrupt?" May 5, 2021, https://www.facebook.com/notes/10218811725070460/

[8] Comment by TS00 on https://heresthejoy.com/2019/08/are-wolves-proliferating-in-the-churches/#comment-200872

The life of the Spirit, in these cases, is optional by default.

Then the wolf can use that strong appeal, often coupled with twisted Scriptures, to set up church people to fulfill their ungodly desires. The epistle of Jude elaborates on this concept.

Is it a common occurrence?

My answer to the questioner at the beginning of this chapter is that I don't know if wolves in the fold was a common occurrence in every stage of history, but sadly I do believe it's a common occurrence now. I believe it will be common as long as . . .

- ➢ Church leaders are unwilling or feel unable to take action against powerful wolves.
- ➢ Christians are asleep to the problem.
- ➢ Fingers are being pointed in the wrong direction.

Pointing fingers in the wrong direction

Speaking of fingers being pointed in the wrong direction, a while back The Gospel Coalition presented us with an article called "Beware of Broken Wolves."[9] The author sought to make a case that people who have been harmed by wolves in our churches or are speaking out about wolves in the church, are themselves the wolves. (I've seen this argument a few times, and even though it doesn't make any sense, it actually gains the desired response more than you might expect.)

That notorious article garnered over 300 comments back in a day when The Gospel Coalition allowed comments on their website. Now, though, all those comments have been removed, perhaps because most of them were saying something like, "Where does the Bible describe broken wolves? That's not who

---

[9] Joe Carter, "Beware of Broken Wolves," *The Gospel Coalition*, April 21, 2017, https://www.thegospelcoalition.org/article/beware-of-broken-wolves/

the real wolves are. The real wolves are in your very own midst, looking like sheep."

In spite of how problematic hundreds of people pointed out this article to be, The Gospel Coalition thought it was good enough to repost again a year later, and as of this writing it still stands on their website with no comments. The problem of abuse in the church by leaders with power—*those who, remember, look like sheep*—is such a very serious one that when a leader points in the wrong direction, I wonder what else is going on. False teachings that set up the vulnerable for abuse are in their very midst, right there in their very own churches. I write about them regularly.[10]

How can a church recognize the wolves?

After listening to scores of stories, I believe that if one who has been accused as a wolf is highly respected, and especially if the wolf is in a position of authority and power . . .

. . . it may be fear that motivates the decision-makers—fear of losing their own position, income, and reputation—or it may be something more sinister. But the majority of church elders appear to be far too inclined to protect the sheep-looking wolf who has prestige, wealth, and above all, power, and too inclined to excommunicate the ones who point out the wolves.

That is, the torn prey, the poor and needy, the widows and orphans, and the "foreigners."

> *Riddle:* How does one recognize a vicious wolf,
> if he looks like a harmless sheep?
> *Answer:* You have to listen to the ones
> who have been harmed by him.

---

[10] For example, see "The Most Important Time to Stop Going to Your Church," *Here's the Joy,* June 17, 2018, https://heresthejoy.com/2018/06/the-most-important-time-to-stop-going-to-your-church-a-response-to-the-gospel-coalition/

If you can't or won't do that, you can expect more and more wolves to be attracted by that invisible "Wolves Welcome" sign over the door.

Watching for the wolves, protecting the sheep

John 10:12-13 says,

> *He who is a hired hand and not a shepherd,*
> *who does not own the sheep,*
> *sees the wolf coming and leaves the sheep and flees,*
> *and the wolf snatches them and scatters them.*
> *He flees because he is a hired hand and cares nothing for the sheep.*

One reader observed,

> *I think many pastors (shepherds) today function more as the hired hand rather than the shepherd described in 1 Peter 5:1-5. They do not know their herd well enough to distinguish the sheep from the wolves or even from the goats.*[11]

There are Christians—some of those who trust and love the Lord Jesus Christ—who are willing to act like Him, as shepherds who look out for the sheep.

I pray that more Christians will be willing to learn how to recognize the breathtakingly hypocritical predators, how to listen to those who have been harmed, how to understand dissociation, and how to gently lead wounded people to Jesus. . . .

. . . instead of bludgeoning them over the head with twisted Scriptures, when they've been wounded by a wolf.

When Jesus said to His disciples, "The harvest truly is plentiful, but the laborers are few" (Luke 10:2), He was referring to the spiritually hungry, needy hearts all around them. Oh, friends, the same is true now. The hungry, needy hearts are all around us. There are those who are desperate to know that God is a good and

---

[11] Donna Welton, personal correspondence, June 27, 2022. Used by permission.

loving God and is Not. Like. Those. Wolves. They need to know that His heart is to rescue, heal, and deliver.

Lord Jesus, send forth laborers into Your harvest. And expose the wolves—and the wolf protectors—in our midst.

UNTWISTED TRUTH FROM CHAPTER 11

- ❖ Jesus, Ezekiel, and Paul all warned about wolves who devour the sheep, amidst the people of God.

- ❖ Wolves come into the church in at least two forms: the Judaizing (law-loving) wolf and the charismatic (attractive and appealing) wolf. They will draw people away from the truth of finding their full salvation in the finished work of Jesus Christ and will draw people to themselves or to lists of rules.

- ❖ In order to identify wolves, Christians must be willing to listen to those who have been harmed by them.

- ❖ True shepherds will want to protect their vulnerable ones from the wolves.

CHAPTER 12

Don't "Err on the Side of Grace"

I suppose that chapter title may sound harsh and judgmental to some. But hang with me here.

"Err on the side of grace" is a maxim brought to my attention by abuse survivors. When I researched, I found it in a large number of books (I stopped counting at 70), and all but two of them expressed the maxim in a positive way. Everywhere it's used, the meaning is basically the same (this is my own synopsis):

> Err on the side of grace.
> Don't judge. Be kind like Jesus. Don't be suspicious. Believe the best of people. Ascribe the best motives to others. You don't know how hard their life is, so be nice. Take them at their word. Take them at face value.
> Err on the side of grace.

Some may use this expression to apply to what we used to call "giving the benefit of the doubt." Outside of any evidence to the contrary, we want to assume that a person means well. For example, when a husband gets home from work late and says it was because of the traffic, if he shows no evidence otherwise of engaging in underhanded practices, the wife would do well to trust him, to give him the benefit of the doubt.

That's not what we're talking about here. Here we're addressing "erring on the side of grace" when there is evidence and/or testimony that something else is going on. Of course, the biggest problem comes when we're dealing with hypocrites, especially those who delight in duping others.

On which side shall we err?

When people say they want to "err on the side of" anything, they're acknowledging that it's easy to make a mistake. When it comes to receiving a show of what's usually known as "repentance"—that is, a show of sadness over the sin and an expressed desire to do better—the ways to err seem to come down to two main possibilities:

You can be *cynical*, refusing to believe anyone who claims this sort of change. Or you can be *gullible*, believing what you're told without question.

In cases like this, when church leaders say they want to "err on the side of grace," what they really mean is that they would rather be gullible than cynical.

Apparently, *gullibility feels more like grace*. But gullibility isn't any more grace than cynicism is.

But this concept of "erring on the side of grace"—which is not grace— can be an attractive option for busy pastors . . .

Because it's easier?

Good church leaders want to see good things happen in the lives of their people. What if someone who has been living a double life "repents," that is, shows sorrow for their misdeeds and says they want to do better? Then those good church leaders can thank God, breathe a sigh of relief, and record a success. That's one more thing wolves are counting on.

But the fact is that "erring on the side of grace" (i.e., gullibility)

➢ doesn't require facing the ugly business of ongoing sin and even evil in our midst.

➤ doesn't require seeking the Holy Spirit.

➤ doesn't require following through to look for the "fruits of repentance"—that is fruits that indicate a life change.[1]

And besides this, there's another important observation that must not be overlooked: "believing the best" about people, that unscriptural command, apparently doesn't work with victims of abuse when they are making accusations. Because "believing the best" apparently always means refusing to believe that the accused could do anything like that.

This decision is certainly the most convenient for the church leader. But it is devastating for the victim.

> *My life demonstrated the fruit of the Spirit, and I had not lived in duplicity. I tried to do everything the pastors/elders had asked. But when I tried to get help from them regarding those who had sex trafficked me as a child, there was no "erring on the side of grace" for me.*
>
> *I and another woman the abusers had trafficked told the elders that the children in their church were at risk. Then the elders said they needed to meet with my abusers to hear their side of the story. We told them the abusers were extremely skilled and would deceive them, but the leaders patted us on our proverbial heads and assured us they would be fine. Of course they were deceived.*
>
> *Then they saw us as the more dangerous ones. Not just one church, but church leaders from four different churches treated me this same way, turning on me, including one famous (or infamous) megachurch.*
>
> *Why does "erring on the side of grace" happen only with abusers? Why is it that they bend over backwards for the wolves while the sheep are left to bleed?*[2]

---

[1] For more about what these "fruits of repentance" will look like, see chapter 14.

[2] Anonymous, personal correspondence, June 24, 2022, used by permission.

What is grace anyway?

As it turns out, "erring on the side of grace" isn't about real grace at all. Grace isn't simply "being nice" or "believing the best." Grace isn't even assuming good intentions. Its meaning doesn't even encompass these other common buzzword uses of the term.

**Grace is the powerful love of God
overflowing from Him by His Holy Spirit,
into and through His people
in a variety of ways that flow out to others.**

God's free-flowing grace will look as varied in different lives as the stories of faith in Hebrews 11. It will look like the lives of Peter and Paul and Philip and Lydia and others, all of whom were called to different missions, but all of whom demonstrated the fruit of the Spirit in their lives. So what does "grace" really encompass? Here are a few pertinent attributes.

Grace encompasses wisdom about evil that can hide in our midst

This is most true in the cases of ones who present themselves as good, even instructors in goodness, while secretly doing evil.

2 Corinthians 11:13-15
For such men
[those who claim they work on the same terms as we do
but are actually serving Satan]
are false apostles, deceitful workmen,
disguising themselves as apostles of Christ.

2 Timothy 3:12-13
Indeed, all who desire to live a godly life in Christ Jesus
will be persecuted,
while evil people and impostors will go on from bad to worse,
deceiving and being deceived.

Grace encourages us to look to the Holy Spirit for discernment

Though none of us is infallible, the Lord has given us prayer and the Holy Spirit to help us in our discernment, especially when it comes to those who look good in public while doing evil in secret.

1 John 4:1
Beloved, do not believe every spirit,
but test the spirits to see whether they are from God:
for many false prophets have gone out into the world.

Ephesians 5:6-17
Let no one deceive you with empty words,
for because of these things the wrath of God comes upon
the sons of disobedience.
Therefore do not become partners with them;
for at one time you were darkness, but now you are light in the Lord.
Walk as children of light
(for the fruit of light is found in all that is good and right and true),
and try to discern what is pleasing to the Lord.
Take no part in the unfruitful works of darkness,
but instead expose them.
For it is shameful even to speak of the things that they do in secret.
But when anything is exposed by the light,
it becomes visible, for anything that becomes visible is light.
Therefore it says, "Awake, O sleeper, and arise from the dead,
and Christ will shine on you."
Look carefully then how you walk, not as unwise but as wise,
making the best use of the time, because the days are evil.
Therefore do not be foolish,
but understand what the will of the Lord is.

Our Lord made it clear over and over again that He expects His people not to be deceived, but to exercise spiritual discernment. For example, when the crowd was angry with Him and He replied to them, He closed with these words in John 7:24,

> *Do not judge by appearances,*
> *but **judge with right judgment.***

Grace directs us to look for "fruits of repentance" and a life of integrity

Jesus said in Matthew 7:15-17,

> *Beware of false prophets, who come to you in sheep's clothing*
> *but inwardly are ravenous wolves.*
> *You will recognize them by their fruits.*
> *Are grapes gathered from thornbushes, or figs from thistles?*
> *So, every healthy tree bears good fruit,*
> *but the diseased tree bears bad fruit.*

Instead of erring on the side of gullibility, those who receive a claim of "repentance" can watch for fruits of repentance (character qualities rather than a to-do checklist), as John the Baptist admonished the Pharisees in Luke 3:8.

Instead of erring on the side of cynicism, those who receive a claim of "repentance" (not just sorrow over sins, but life change) can be hopeful, that God will be at work in the lives of at least some of those who make the claim and that their lives will eventually bring forth the "fruits of repentance."

The "fruits of repentance"? They'll look like the fruit of the Spirit in Galatians 5:22-25.

> *Being nice, polite, and uninvolved in others' traumas is NOT a fruit of the Spirit. One of the most destructive pastors I had the misfortune of knowing was a very polite, nice guy. You'd love him as a neighbor. He'd mow your lawn; help you move; support any sexual abuser who could utter the words, "I'm sorry, I've changed"; verbally bully concerned church members out the door; and politely slander them after they left.*[3]

---

[3] Anonymous, personal correspondence, June 23, 2022. Used by permission.

CHAPTER 12 – DON'T "ERR ON THE SIDE OF GRACE"

The fruit of the Spirit will come out of a life of integrity. That life will look very different, even in private and secret, from the lusts of the flesh described in Galatians 5:19-21.

The life of integrity will be lived the same in public, in private, and in secret.[4]

Grace produces wisdom that is neither gullible nor cynical

In Matthew 10:16 Jesus said,

Behold, I am sending you out as sheep in the midst of wolves, so be wise as serpents and innocent as doves.

Being "innocent as doves" does not mean being gullible. It simply means living a life of purity, an attribute the doves represented. And of course, being "wise as serpents" does not mean being cynical. It means being alert and circumspect and careful.

Being pure in our actions and thoughts as well as being alert and careful—Jesus made it clear that those two qualities can exist together in harmony. In fact, stated slightly differently, these are among the attributes required of elders in the church, according to Titus 1:6-9 and 1 Timothy 3:1-7.

However, sadly, in their desire to be as innocent as doves, many Christians have become as wise as sitting ducks. Rather than "erring on the side of grace," they err on the side of foolishness. Then they become suspicious of—and condemning of—the wrong people. For example,

I am surrounded by churches who choose to "err on the side of grace." All my abusers are "given grace" while the onus has been on me to just keep on smiling. And they wonder why I don't feel

---

[4] For more about this, see "5 Reasons for Church Small Groups to Replace Transparency with Integrity," *Here's the Joy,* May 17, 2018, https://heresthejoy.com/2018/05/5-reasons-for-church-small-groups-to-replace-transparency-with-integrity/

safe or welcome in their congregations? Besides the deep wounds of ongoing abuse, I am expected to accept the spiritual abuse of the churches.[5]

But does the alternative mean that we have to be willing to "believe the worst"? Actually yes, sometimes it does. After all, among other pertinent Scriptures, Jude warns us (verse 4),

> *For certain people have crept in unnoticed*
> *who long ago were designated for this condemnation,*
> *ungodly people,*
> **who pervert the grace of our God into sensuality**
> *and deny our only Master and Lord, Jesus Christ.*

So we approach the subject with this understanding, even as we seek the Lord for wisdom and seek to truly listen with compassion to those who say they have been harmed. No matter what we ultimately conclude about any individual, it means we need to treat those who come for help with love and care rather than casting them out, as has happened to so many.

That's not to say that if Christians truly do seek to fully follow the Lord, we will never be deceived. We're fallible, and wolves in sheep's clothing can be extremely deceptive. But we can determine to prayerfully seek the guidance of the Holy Spirit and gain more understanding about the ways the wicked operate. We can learn not only from the Scriptures but also from those who have experience with wolves.

We can be watchful and on guard even as we live lives of purity before God. Innocent as doves, but also wise as serpents.

What does it mean to "look for evidences of grace"?

In the same vein as "erring on the side of grace," some church leaders have determined that we should "look for evidences of

---

[5] Healinginhim, comment on https://heresthejoy.com/2017/11/erring-on-the-side-of-grace-when-it-comes-to-repentance/#comment-189733

grace" even in the lives of abusers. A reader described to me how her church conducted marriage counseling: the married couple had been told to come up with a list of "evidences of grace" that they saw in each other's lives.

> *We were to say them out loud in front of each other and the elders meeting with us. They were, after all, constantly reminding us that Scripture called us to "believe the best" of each other, and this exercise was meant to help us do that.*[6]

This woman came up with an impressive list of good things her husband was doing. But there was another list that was also true.

> *They knew I was sincere. They knew I loved him–and the Lord. Surely that meant they would take my other list seriously, the one I had shared with them on that first trembling phone call in the middle of a dark parking lot at night?*[7]

I'm guessing many readers here could add their own stories of abusers who showed what this church called "evidences of grace." One man I know of who was selling his children for others to abuse, at the same time was an impressive example in his church when it comes to these "evidences." If his wife had gone for marriage counseling (which she didn't, because she was too controlled), the list of "evidences of grace" she could have given would have bowled you over. She could have rightly said her husband . . .

➢ Is a deacon/elder
➢ Teaches adult Sunday school and preaches sometimes
➢ Leads singing, sings in the choir, and sings special music
➢ Helps with VBS
➢ Helps with bus ministry

---

[6] "Looking for Evidences of Grace in the Life of an Abuser," *Here's the Joy,* November 27, 2018, https://heresthejoy.com/2018/11/looking-for-evidences-of-grace-in-the-life-of-an-abuser. (The Scriptures never call us to do that.)
[7] Ibid.

- Helps in youth group
- Leads in kids' programs
- Works in the nursery
- Helps clean the church building
- Participates in church work days
- Plays basketball, volleyball, and other sports with the young people after services.

Church leaders will use the term "evidences of grace" to describe a list they want to see kept, a series of hoops they want their church members to jump through. But the teachings of the New Covenant in which we live say nothing about keeping a list or jumping through any church-declared hoops.

What "works" will these "false apostles and deceitful workers" be judged by, at the end? It won't be that list that satisfied the church leaders. It will be the works that spilled out of the heart in the secret places.

As it turned out, the woman with the "other list" for her elders was not believed. They told her she was speaking evil of her husband, biting and devouring, exaggerating, and telling falsehoods.[8]

After all, those false religious leaders Jesus talked about had those "evidences of grace" in their lives too. They tithed. They prayed in public. They knew the law and could probably recite it backwards in their sleep. But Jesus called them wolves because of that "other list."

> *It astounds me how the "evidences of grace" for these elders all revolve around church activity. One of the huge red flags that point to a misunderstanding of the gospel is the belief that "doing church" is what the Christian is called to. That's a pretty low bar, one that many abusers can handle quite easily.*
>
> *The real fruits of a child of God, as you suggest, revolve around a spirit and expression of selfless love. Ticking off a list of church activities does not even begin to suggest the Spirit of Christ within*

---

[8] Ibid.

a person. No one "did church," or apparent righteousness, better than those who Jesus called "vipers" and "whited sepulchers."

When the spouses and families of the leading, most beloved, friendliest, most helpful elder and servants of the church assert "what big teeth they have" at home, we need to start looking for zippers in their sheep costume.[9]

Who suffers when we pervert the meaning of "grace"?

When I asked my readers to review this chapter, I received some strong and heartfelt responses. Here is one:

> *A big part of my journey has been healing from the trauma responses my body gave me to any discussion about "grace." I could see it in Scripture, but the way I'd experienced it was that this "grace" was for abusers, not me. Grace did not functionally exist for me. Expectations, scrutiny, and criticism were for victims. I couldn't even grieve. Grace was second chances (to do what?), and if I couldn't offer that to abusers, I was the problem.*[10]

God's outpouring of grace will result in others being cared for well as the Name of the Lord is lifted up. If Christians want to protect the most vulnerable of God's people, they must be willing to gain a true and robust understanding of what "grace" really is. And they need to give serious, prayerful consideration to accusations of gross hypocrisy in the lives of church people—even the lives of their most "exemplary" church members and leaders.

The God of grace wants the wolves exposed.

---

[9] TS00, comment on https://heresthejoy.com/2018/11/looking-for-evidences-of-grace-in-the-life-of-an-abuser/#comment-196740

[10] Rhoda Hostetler, personal correspondence, June 24, 2022. Used by permission.

UNTWISTED TRUTH FROM CHAPTER 12

- ❖ "Believing the best" about anyone is not commanded in Scripture. Instead we can give the benefit of the doubt in questionable situations when there is no evidence or testimony to the contrary.

- ❖ We should be neither cynical nor gullible in interacting with others. We should be led by the Holy Spirit in wisdom.

- ❖ "Erring on the side of grace" (that is, gullibility) avoids facing the ugly business of ongoing sin and even evil in our midst, seeking the Holy Spirit, or looking for the "fruits of repentance"—that is, fruits that indicate a life change.

- ❖ Grace from God encompasses the wisdom that recognizes that evil hides in our midst.

- ❖ Grace from God encourages us to look to the Holy Spirit for discernment.

- ❖ Grace from God directs us to look for fruits of repentance and a life of integrity.

- ❖ Grace from God produces wisdom that is neither gullible nor cynical.

- ❖ The evidence of God's work in one's life is the fruit of the Spirit, described in Galatians 5:22-25.

- ❖ The life of integrity will be lived the same in public, in private, and in secret.

CHAPTER 13

Jesus vs. the Vipers

When you read the Gospels, asking the Lord to open your eyes to see them as if you were reading them for the first time, you might get a whole new perspective on the big clash between Jesus and the Jewish religious leaders, the scribes and Pharisees and priests.

What were those Jewish religious leaders like?

They've been misrepresented, you know, those scribes, Pharisees, and priests. Almost every time they're portrayed or described, we think about them as obviously pompous, arrogant, and hypocritical. But their hypocrisy wasn't obvious to most of the Jewish people.

You think, perhaps, that this is because they were naïve, and you wouldn't have been so naïve? Well, maybe not. But perhaps there are some among us today who have been deceived by church leaders today, who to our shock we have found to be hypocrites. Perhaps we've been deceived by leaders who claimed to be building a kingdom for the Savior, only to find out that all along they were building a kingdom for themselves.

Yes, I raise my hand. Over and over. I've been deceived again and again by leaders that I thought truly followed Jesus Christ, who turned out to be breathtaking hypocrites. That's how good they are at the games they play.

And the religious leaders in Jesus' world were just that good.

This is why the crowds were shocked—*shocked*—when during His 3.5 years of public ministry, Jesus called out the religious leaders as vipers, whited sepulchers, blind leaders of the blind, and more.

> *I am new to the world of exposing false teaching. I am not new to the world of false shepherds.*
>
> *I have observed that many leaders are building their own kingdom, not the Kingdom of God. In order to do that, they must keep their people dependent and fearful and full of false humility.*
>
> *Confidence in God and our position in Christ is the greatest threat to the kingdom of man. Believe, but not too much. Pray, but pray cautiously. God is your father, but He is distant. Just show up, give your tithe, and do not question anything.*
>
> *These incorrect teachings have "life" among God's people because we as a generation have ceased to think for ourselves. It's much easier to be spoon fed by anyone who exudes authority.*[1]

The two governments

In those days, the Jews had two sets of governments. The Roman overlords were the hated foreigners (picture Nazi Germany having conquered us in World War 2 and our street corners swarming with German soldiers).

But as much as the Jews hated the Romans, the Roman government stayed out of Jewish religious affairs. Though it was technically illegal for them to kill anyone, if the Jews had wanted to hold a lynching because someone claimed to be a messiah figure, the Roman soldiers would have turned the other way, as long as the mob didn't get too unruly.

---

[1] Anonymous, personal correspondence, March 28, 2022, used by permission.

Basically, as long as the Jews obeyed Roman law, most of the Romans just didn't care what they believed or practiced.

When Jesus was arrested and brought to the Roman governor Pilate, the Roman soldiers did indeed take advantage of the opportunity to mock and torture a man who couldn't defend himself: they were the ones who applied the crown of thorns and the purple robe, spitting in His face, slapping and beating Him.

But they did that simply because they were bullies. It wasn't because they knew who He was; they didn't. Like any bullies, they simply saw an opportunity to hurt a defenseless man for fun. When it came right down to it, they didn't care one way or another about a solitary man who wasn't stirring up any trouble.

And that brings us to that other government. The religious leaders.

The midnight criminals

Who was the crowd who came for Jesus in the middle of the night? Those weren't Roman soldiers. They were the lackeys of the religious leaders and even some of the religious leaders themselves. The ones who knew who He was.

Gang violence was perpetrated against Jesus before the assault perpetrated by the Roman soldiers. In my previous *Untwisting Scriptures* book I wrote about the midnight secret trial conducted by the kangaroo court these religious leaders so craftily set up.[2] Mark 14:65 and Luke 22:63-65 tell us that it was the "godly" religious leaders who spat on Him and struck Him and mocked Him.

That is the depths to which they sank.

And my guess is, they would go out the next day and smoothly instruct their disciples in the finer points of what it means to honor God with their lives.

Because the best hypocrites are amazing like that.

---

[2] *Untwisting Scriptures that were used to tie you up, gag you, and tangle your mind: Book 3 Your Words, Your Emotions,* Pennycress Publishing, 2021, pp 65-66.

And oh, did I say secret trial? When I read the account in the Gospels, my mind flashed to a secret trial held over a friend of mine, a group of men against her, proclaiming judgment against her because she had reported her abusive husband. (But they are highly respected religious leaders, with many truly adoring followers.)

You may know of other secret meetings at which those who are highly respected have done terrible things to the innocent ones. These innocent ones are those who have shared in the sufferings of Jesus, the perfectly innocent one.

The depths to which they sank

These highly respected leaders—respected by followers who were no more naïve than many of us have been—are the ones who decided that Jesus should die because He was usurping their place, attracting their followers to Himself. And they decided that they wanted Him to die in the most excruciating and ignominious way possible, simply because they hated Him that much.

That's why they didn't arrange for thugs to kill Him in the night, which would have been so much simpler. That's why they aroused the crowd, so Pilate would condemn a man *that he knew was innocent* to hang on a Roman cross for public mockery.

This is the depth of darkness these leaders were in already: when Judas came back to tell them Jesus was innocent (Matthew 27), their reply was, basically, "Why are you talking about that? That's not our problem. That's your problem."

You think we care about guilt and innocence? Oh hahaha.

You've suddenly developed a conscience? That just gets in the way around here.

Oh, he's returning the money we gave him to betray his friend to death? Well, it's "blood money," so we won't put that in the temple fund, but we can use it to buy that sweet piece of property over there.

We will "keep the law"—mint, rue, anise, micro-doctrine that we elevate to the level of salvation—but we will arrogantly (behind the scenes, of course, in secret and in the cover of darkness) thumb our noses at justice, mercy, and truth.

Mint, rue, and anise can be seen and measured. Laws pertaining to outward appearances fit in the visible, measurable micro-doctrine status. You only need to glance at an individual to judge them by those measures. But justice, mercy, and faithfulness? You have to sit with people, to know their stories well, to judge by those measures. The Pharisees weren't willing to sit with others in their pain. It wasn't necessary in their approach.

The Pharisees loved the law and hated the prophets, while convincing themselves they loved the prophets. Jesus called their bluff in Matthew 23:29-32. They loved laws because laws meant power, prestige, and recognition; they even built extra laws around God's law. But the prophets rejected personal applause and pointed forward to Another, they broke laws and norms (like Hosea marrying Gomer or Jonah going to Nineveh), and they identified with society's rejects in true prophetic calls back to God's heart. Had the Pharisees truly loved and heard the prophets, they'd have recognized Jesus as the fulfillment of prophecy, as God with us.[3]

Truly this is why Jesus said during the midnight arrest (in Luke 22:53), "But this is your hour, and the power of darkness."

It was the power of darkness—devilish, satanic power—fueling these men, for all their humble looks and unctuous sermons and pious admonitions and sanctimonious prayers in the streets.

He knew that, even when He called them out, publicly, in the streets of Jerusalem. He reserved his strongest language for these religious leaders who looked good on the outside, who acted holy in public. The same ones who laid rule after rule on the backs of the people, but in secret were "vipers" and "full of dead men's

---

[3] Rhoda Hostetler, personal correspondence, June 24, 2022. Used by permission.

bones." But they refused to be corrected, considering their minutiae of outward-rule-keeping to be their ticket to holiness.

You can read His scathing "woes" to these hypocrites in Matthew 23. Here's just a sampling from verses 13-33, and remember, Jesus pronounced woes like these on *no other group of people.*

Woe to you, scribes and Pharisees, hypocrites!
For you shut the kingdom of heaven in people's faces.
For you neither enter yourselves
nor allow those who would enter to go in.
Woe to you, scribes and Pharisees, hypocrites!
For you devour widows' houses
and for a pretense you make long prayers;
therefore you will receive the greater condemnation.
For you travel across sea and land to make a single proselyte,
and when he becomes a proselyte,
you make him twice as much a child of hell as yourselves.
For you tithe mint and dill and cumin,
and have neglected the weightier matters of the law:
justice and mercy and faithfulness.
These you ought to have done, without neglecting the others.
You blind guides, straining out a gnat and swallowing a camel!
For you clean the outside of the cup and the plate,
but inside they are full of greed and self-indulgence.
You blind Pharisee!
First clean the inside of the cup and the plate,
that the outside also may be clean.
For you are like whitewashed tombs,
which outwardly appear beautiful,
but within are full of dead people's bones and all uncleanness.
So you also outwardly appear righteous to others,
but within you are full of hypocrisy and lawlessness.
You serpents, you brood of vipers,
how are you to escape being sentenced to hell?

Jesus knew, all along. He knew exactly how it was all going to shake out. He knew that the visceral, devilish hatred of the "godly" religious leaders would lead to His death.

He knew.

And He moved forward anyway, doing what His Father had called Him to do, facing the horror and staring it down.

He is our wonderful, beautiful, strong, and loving Example and Savior. In spite of the religious leaders who try to block the way, we can still run to Him. He wins in the end.

UNTWISTED TRUTH FROM CHAPTER 13

- ❖ The scribes, Pharisees, and priests were brilliantly deceptive at the double-life game they played. Many modern hypocrites are just as brilliant in their hypocrisy.
- ❖ The only "woes" Jesus proclaimed were upon the massively hypocritical Jewish religious leaders.
- ❖ Jesus wins in the end.

PART FOUR

We Can Flourish in Our Christian Lives

CHAPTER 14

Why "Metanoia" Is So Much Greater Than "Repentance"—and Why That's Important

In the Middle Ages when monks had access to the New Testament, it was in the Latin translation called the Vulgate. They would see that John the Baptist and Jesus called out to their hearers, *"Do penance! For the Kingdom of heaven is at hand!"*

Really? Did John the Baptist and Jesus really call for their hearers to achieve absolution for sin through acts of self-mortification, confession to a priest, contrition, and other similar practices?

But as it turns out, the meaning of the original Greek word *metanoia* doesn't involve doing any acts of piety. Rather, we learn, it means "change your mind."

What does the "change of mind" mean? And why would I agree with some great thinkers that *repentance* is not an acceptable translation? And why do I believe this truth is vitally important for all of us?

Not long ago I was directed to the old book *The Great Meaning of Metanoia*, by Treadwell Walden. To my delight I found that it agreed with and even expanded on my own thoughts when I first wrote about "repentance" years ago.[1]

The first cry of John the Baptist (Matthew 3:2) and the first cry of Jesus are both translated in English as, "Repent! For the Kingdom of Heaven is at hand!" But since we're exploring the word *metanoia* here, I'm going to use that word instead.

Can we approach the Scriptures afresh? Can we look at them asking the Holy Spirit to clear away any meaning that is not from Him and show us what they really mean?

Metanoia! For the Kingdom of Heaven is at hand!

It is clearly an important word, heralding as it did the Kingdom of God. Many other "new" words made an appearance in the New Testament as well.

> *... Expressions conveying a divine meaning, now most familiar to us, were occasions of astonishment to pagan and Jew alike when they were lifted into connections which transfigured them. Such, we know, were "faith," "hope," "love," "light," "truth," "life," "peace," "liberty"; such were "redemption," "atonement," "righteousness," "resurrection"; such were "Saviour" and "apostle," and many more which might be named. And such was "Metanoia."*[2]

Metanoia, the great harbinger of the kingdom

Though the word *metanoia* in the Greek literally means "a change of mind," this is more than a logical "I see your point." Or a whimsical "I guess I'll do something else instead."

---

[1] "What Does Real Repentance Look Like?" *Here's the Joy*, December 9, 2012, https://heresthejoy.com/2012/12/come-to-your-senses/

[2] Treadwell Walden, *The Great Meaning of Metanoia: An Undeveloped Chapter in the Life and Teaching of Christ*, Thomas Whittaker, 1896, p 12.

CHAPTER 14 – WHY "METANOIA" IS SO MUCH GREATER THAN "REPENTANCE"

No, there is something deeper about it. This "change of mind" indicates *opening the understanding leading to transformation.*

"Metanoia" was the great harbinger word of the Gospel, bearing witness to the "Light."[3]

It is as if our Lord said to His listeners, "I have come to completely change your world. I am here to change your paradigm. Open your mind, your heart, your eyes. Listen and receive understanding in the deepest places of yourself."

"We are showing you a new thing. A new kingdom is entering. Allow your thinking to be transformed, and see it!"

Jesus proclaimed, "Metanoia! Come to your senses! For God's Kingdom is here!" Our Lord Jesus was welcoming all who would hear, all who would see, into nothing less than a new life. Not a new life of A New List of Rules, but a new life of Everything is Different.

The people who walked in darkness have seen a great light.
Those who dwelt in a land of deep darkness,
on them has light shone.[4]

The metanoia Jesus offered

For three years, our Lord Jesus made good on His proclamation/command of "metanoia." He did new things. He performed miracles the likes of which hadn't been seen in Israel since the days of Elijah. He taught in a completely new way. All who heard were astonished. For some, those who had ears to hear, the Truth sank in like water on thirsty ground.

He spoke in parables. He used His miracles as metaphors. He used nature as object lessons. He spoke sometimes in dark

---

[3] Ibid., p 37.
[4] Isaiah 9:2, quoted in Matthew 4:16.

statements, sometimes in plain language. But He was always teaching, always leading "those with ears to hear" to the truth proclaimed by His "Metanoia."

**The Lord Jesus Christ
is the Beginning and Ending of this New Era.
He is the Answer to all the Law and the Prophets.
He is the Proclaimer of the Way
that Moses could see only in shadow.**

Through His words and His works, He demonstrated His worthiness to be the Herald of this New Kingdom. Through His death, resurrection, and ascension, He accomplished the ultimate work of this New Covenant.

When Jesus rose from the dead, the disciples' metanoia entered upon a new stage. Their "sorrow was turned into joy," as He had predicted in John 16:20-22. Now they would set their minds and affections on things above, not on things of this earth.[5]

The great transformation

What would be the natural result of "metanoia"? It would be the highest form of faith—faith in the Lord Jesus Christ as the Savior, not only from death, but for the new life He promises.

There is Great Truth. Metanoia, that "coming to your senses," brings about the revelation, the experience of that Great Truth. When that Great Truth is experienced, seen, known through metanoia, then the result is Faith.

Many believe they have faith because they have assented to a set of facts and have tried to deal with their sin. And many of them do have faith, after a manner of speaking. But they have not had the great metanoia of the soul that is the opening of the eyes to who Jesus really is.

---

[5] Colossians 3:1-4.

Paul did, and he was never the same. On the road to Damascus, Paul was fundamentally transformed. Paul, in fact, had an Experience: he saw and heard the Risen Lord. As soon as he did, he was on his face, and there was no turning back. The metanoia that Jesus proclaimed at the beginning of His ministry, Paul experienced. It was this deep, all-encompassing transformation that he preached.

This "change of mind" explains at least in part the energy and enthusiasm with which Paul accomplished all he did. This "change of mind" explains the raptures he experienced when describing the risen Lord of glory. This "change of mind" illuminated and affected his entire self, his deepest nature, never to be the same, ever again.

When Paul told this conversion story to King Agrippa, he added that the Lord Jesus said He was sending him (Paul) to the Gentiles (Acts 26:18),

to open their eyes,
so that they may turn from darkness to light
and from the power of Satan to God.

This is metanoia.

Paul then told King Agrippa more about these people, that he "declared . . . that they should *repent* and turn to God, performing deeds in keeping with their *repentance*" (Acts 26:20).

Do you immediately think "they should be sorry for their sins" and "they should do deeds that show they're truly sorry"? But that isn't what this word means. Instead, you can read it this way: Paul

*declared that they should **come to their senses** and turn to God,*
receiving a whole new way of thinking and being,
*and then produce the fruit that comes from **such a transformation**.*

The "repentance" translation fail

All that I wrote above, much of it based on Walden's book, is the same conclusion I had reached back when I wrote that first article about this word. This is why back then I paraphrased Jesus as saying, "Come to your senses!"[6]

But where does the word *repentance* come from, the word that has been used to translate *metanoia* in almost every English version of the Bible?

It's one more contribution to confusion about the gospel.

While *metanoia* is Greek, *repentance* comes from the Latin word *poenitentia*, from *poena*, "pain." They are almost completely unrelated words.[7]

Three English words come from the Latin word that emphasizes the pain one would feel (or inflict on oneself) because of sin.

Penance—self-punishment done in order to get back in favor with God.

Penitence—contrition, sorrow for sins, usually associated with doing penance in order to get back into God's favor.

Repentance—contrition, sorrow for sins.[8]

This word *repentance* is inextricably linked to pain or suffering:

> *Suffering in view of being liable to punishment; hence grief over an act for which satisfaction might be demanded. It would be fair to allow it also a secondary signification; suffering in view of the badness of the act itself, without regard to its consequences.*
>
> *The prefix re, "back" or "again," adds to this the idea of looking back, or looking again, with sorrow upon what has been done amiss.*
>
> *The word thus intensively communes with the past, and represents an emotion only.*[9]

Walden expresses some reasons the word *repentance* can never adequately substitute for the word *metanoia*:

---

[6] "What Does Real Repentance Look Like?" *Here's the Joy*.

[7] If you find history and etymology as fascinating as I do, you may be interested to read Walden's account on pages 108-122 of his book about the journey involved in replacing *metanoia* (a word focusing on the mind or understanding) with *repentance* (a word focusing on pain).

[8] In Catholic theology, this word is synonymous with penitence. In Protestant theology, acts of penance are not usually included.

[9] Walden, p 14, emphasis added.

> *It contains undying reminiscence of vengeance, punishment, and expiation. It carries an undying suggestion that the Change of Mind is only a change of will wrought by fear.*
>
> *With undying determination, it presents a theory of radical corruption in which tears are an all-powerful cleansing agent....*
>
> *It has put upon the face of God the frown of outraged justice.*[10]

And indeed, though his book was written in 1895, I have to say that the meaning of the word has changed not at all since then. I've read material from modern luminaries that express this same sentiment.

> *The note of [repentance] is not of emancipation, but of condemnation.... The working of it is not joyful, but sorrowful. Its face is turned in horror towards sin, not in rapture towards righteousness.... It flees the evil in fear of "penalty"—of the punitive action of God or of its own conscience....*
>
> *In its effective operation it can take hold of the Mind, change the mental attitude, determine the mental purpose, but it can never alone renew the whole spiritual constitution of the Mind.*[11]

Contrasting "repentance" with "metanoia"

> *Was the major proclamation of Jesus and the apostles "Repent! Feel sorry for your sins!"? Or was it "Metanoia! Think a new way!"? Do you see what a difference these two words make?*[12]

Since Jesus cried out, in effect, "Come to your senses! Change your understanding! You blind eyes, see! You deaf ears, hear!" then can we see that this *metanoia* is far bigger than simply being sorry for our sins and asking forgiveness? Is that not making the gospel too small?

---

[10] Ibid., pp 125-26, paraphrased.

[11] Ibid., pp 105-06.

[12] Eli Brayley, "The Great Meaning of Metanoia," *Timothy Ministry,* July 26, 2012. https://web.archive.org/web/20220331111755/http://www.timothyministry.com/2012/07/the-great-meaning-of-metanoia.html

Metanoia can encompass "repentance," but the terms are by no means equal, since metanoia introduces a more expansive paradigm than "be scared and sorry for your badness."

> *Of "Metanoia," as Jesus used the word, the lamenting one's sins was a small part; the main part was something far more active and fruitful, the setting up an immense new inward movement for obtaining the rule of life. And "metanoia," accordingly, is a change of the inward man.*[13]

Though turning from sin is part of the Christian life, it is only a small part of what metanoia is about. In fact the New Kingdom that Jesus proclaimed with His call for "Metanoia" was and is a kingdom in which the power of sin is destroyed. –

> *It means a movement of the whole mind forwards, to which a looking backwards is only incidental.*[14]

**Metanoia is as far greater than
"weep and wail so that God might have mercy on you"
as an eagle is greater than a sparrow.**

What is lost when the word *repentance* is used in place of *metanoia*? Walden says,

> *The all-encompassing grandeur of an announcement which takes in the whole of life and calls upon man*
> *– to enlarge his consciousness with the eternal and the spiritual,*
> *– to live on the scale of another life,*
> *– to let his character grow under this great knowledge,*
> *– to let his conduct fall into the lines of the revealed divine will, all this is lost.*[15]

---

[13] Walden., p 93.
[14] Ibid., p 15.
[15] Ibid., p 24.

CHAPTER 14 – WHY "METANOIA" IS SO MUCH GREATER THAN "REPENTANCE"

In 2 Corinthians 7:9 Paul wrote to the Corinthian Christians,

> *I rejoice, not because you were grieved [over your sin],*
> *but because you were grieved into repenting*
> *[metanoia—a complete transformation of mind*
> *leading to a transformation of the life].*
> *For you felt a godly grief, so that you suffered no loss through us.*

Godly sorrow over sin is that sorrow which leads to metanoia, coming to the senses. Peter, Zacchaeus, and the "woman who was a sinner," all were aware of their sinfulness before the Holy One of God. That will be true for everyone who comes to Him. But what He invites us to is beyond the constant cycle of awareness of and forgiveness of sins. He invites us all to come to our senses and enter an entirely new way of thinking and being.

> *John's baptism, we read in our Bibles, was a "baptism of repentance for the remission of sins." We think then, that the people were sorry for their sins and afraid of God's judgment.*
>
> *But that is not what it says. John's baptism was a "baptism of metanoia." It was a baptism signaling, heralding the transformation of life that was to come. Those who were baptized signaled their desire to enter into the new way that this wilderness prophet was heralding. John's baptism was for the "sending away" of sins—the natural effect is to set the soul free from the bondage of the disposition to sin.*[16]

When metanoia becomes a reality in a life, sins are sent away. They no longer have power over us.

And now the difficulty with "Why would Jesus receive a baptism that was all about being sorry for sins?" falls away. That wasn't what it was about at all. The baptism of Jesus was about this transformation of life that Jesus would also be calling His listeners to. And He would not only call them to it, but *He would provide it.*

---

[16] Ibid., p 49.

You've seen the lack

God never designed the Christian life to be simply a cycle of sin-sorry-struggle-sin-sorry-struggle, which is what is preached in so many churches.

Metanoia has in view the mind and understanding, the spiritual eyes, the heart, the life. Yes, sin will be gotten out of the way so we can see, know, and experience our Lord Jesus and His power in our lives. But when there is a new awareness, a new experience, a person's heart will turn toward the Lord without striving.

You have perhaps seen some of these things in the church you came from. You may not have grasped—as I certainly didn't—how much the import of the word *repentance*, as substituted for *metanoia*, played a part.

Listen to what Walden said about the churches of his day.

> *Despite himself, the reader hears the "Repent ye!" of John the Baptist and of the Saviour, like a cry, a note of danger, full of terror, amid which the hearts of the people stood still, instead of what it really was, the invocation of a mind, heart, and life which should befit such a glad and glorious "change" as the kingdom of heaven on earth. . . .*
>
> *This supposed appeal to the impenitent nature only has been taken up as the burden of all preaching, all spiritual counsel; an appeal in their hands often wrought up with terrific penal imagery; and then the fright which has ensued and its consequences have been accepted as the change of heart. . . .*
>
> *There is a tendency to regard an emotional condition, a general passion of religious feeling, however induced, as the seat of efficacy with God, and as the only safe and promising state in which to be and continue in the Christian life.* [17]

This is still so true over 125 years later.

---

[17] Ibid., pp 21-23.

CHAPTER 14 – WHY "METANOIA" IS SO MUCH GREATER THAN "REPENTANCE"

You see the possibility of abundance

> *The real power of the new life lies in looking forward, not backward. It lies in faith, not fear. In knowledge, not sorrow.*
>
> *It is awakening to righteousness and **therefore** sinning not. . . .*
>
> *Metanoia is a word profound enough to describe the mightiest motive that could energize the nature of man, that is, the personal power of the Son of God.*
>
> *It expounds the mightiest influence that could enter his inmost being to the upbuilding of his character and life, namely, the inspiration of the Spirit of God.*[18]

Though I didn't fully understand this concept of metanoia and how much greater it is than "repentance," through the years I did cry out for the Lord to open my eyes and help me know Him. Through the years, through a series of epiphanies He has done that and continues to do that. Sometimes (not always) the opening of my eyes has included sorrow over my sin.

If you came out of abuse of any kind, you may have longed for your abuser(s) to "repent"—to be sorry for their sins. At the same time you may feel frustration that the "repentance" you want to see is too easy for a hard-hearted imposter to fake in the short term.

But the metanoia that Jesus and the apostles talked about—that is a beautiful gift, available to each one of us who asks. In fact, if you grew up in a rule-centered church, an authority-driven church, a penitence-oriented church, you may be longing for something more. Maybe you want to cry out for metanoia too.

> "Lord, I want to really know You.
> Give me the changing of the mind,
> the opening of the understanding."

Grant me metanoia.

---

[18] Ibid., p 137, paraphrase.

When the metanoia of God happens within us, then the dream goal of being fully satisfied with Him in our spirits is accomplished within us. So many of the teachings of the gospels and the epistles will be filled with new and deeper meaning.

Our understanding of the entire New Testament—the unfolding of the New Covenant in which we live—will be transformed when we understand what Jesus was crying out when He called out, "Metanoia!"

It can be a journey, yes, especially if we're unlearning what has been ingrained for decades. But we can anticipate that eventually we will fully understand with Paul what he joyfully proclaimed in so many places in the New Testament, like this one in 2 Corinthians 4:6.

For God, who said,
"Let light shine out of darkness,"
has shone in our hearts
to give the light of the knowledge of the glory of God
in the face of Jesus Christ.

Metanoia.

CHAPTER 14 – WHY "METANOIA" IS SO MUCH GREATER THAN "REPENTANCE"

UNTWISTED TRUTH FROM CHAPTER 14

- ❖ The word *repentance* has a very different meaning than the Greek word it is supposed to translate, *metanoia*.

- ❖ *Metanoia* is not a word of condemnation or threats of punishment. It is a "change of mind" that indicates an opening of the understanding that leads to transformation.

- ❖ Repentance indicates looking *back* at sin and feeling *pain* over it. It strikes a note of threats of punishment and condemnation.

- ❖ Metanoia indicates understanding something you previously did not understand. It strikes a note of beauty, joy, and glory.

- ❖ In the early part of their ministries, both Jesus and John the Baptist declared, "Metanoia!" Not "weep and wail over your sins," but "come to your senses!" or "think a new way!"

- ❖ Examples of the great meaning of metanoia can be found in Matthew 4:16, Acts 26:18, and 2 Corinthians 4:6.

CHAPTER 15

Free From Sin

Romans 6:17-18
But thanks be to God that you who were once slaves of sin,
have become obedient from the heart
to the standard [pattern] of teaching to which you were committed,
and, having been set free from sin,
have become slaves of righteousness.

It's important, in any discussion of sin, to understand the people groups we're talking about, according to which "kingdom" they're in and who they're looking to for help.

First are those who have moved from the kingdom of darkness to the Kingdom of God's dear Son, Jesus Christ.[1]

Some of these born-again believers who love God are still bound up with false beliefs and twisted Scriptures, trying to live the Christian life by their own efforts "in the flesh," as the Bible says. They have trusted Jesus Christ for a change of eternal destination, but they don't understand how to trust Christ fully for a day-to-day change of the life.[2] Thus, if they are honest believers who want to please God, the Christian life will seem like a long, hard struggle.

---

[1] Colossians 1:13, KJV.

[2] For much more on this, see *Prayer Armor for Defense Against the Enemy's Flaming Darts,* Pennycress Publishing, 2019, especially pp 19-21 and pp 113-115.

Some of these born-again believers who love God are walking in faith by the power of His Holy Spirit, aware that the life God has freely offered us can be accomplished only through Him.

There are plenty of us on the journey from one end to the other, untwisting more and more Scriptures and getting to see more and more clearly who Jesus really is and who we really are in Him. It is a deeply worthwhile process, even when there is sometimes pain and loss along the way.

Then there are those who are in the kingdom of darkness. The Bible uses many different words to name them, but to keep things a little simpler here, I'll mention only "the lost" and "the wicked."

The "lost" are not necessarily malicious but are blinded to the truth of the salvation offered them through our Lord Jesus Christ. They make life choices with no regard as to whether these choices are in line with the heart of God. They do not know Him and they do not care about Him one way or another. They go their own way.

The "wicked" are depicted in the Scriptures with no overtones of being attractive, the way the word has been perverted today. The wicked in Scripture are those whose hearts are set against God, as if they are shaking their fists in His face.

The differences among these groups of people are often not even distinguished in churches today, and in many churches, believers are regularly treated as if we are "the wicked." But these differences are vital to understand, especially when it comes to sin.

Sin in the life of a Christian walking in the Spirit

The Christian who trusts Jesus Christ for all his righteousness is, according to Romans 6:18, free from sin. This means that we are not bound to it, are not enslaved by it. This means when sin does enter the life, we will have ears to hear the voice of the Holy Spirit—through the Scriptures, through another person, or through intimate heart connection. We may have life-and-death struggles with sins and temptations, but we will turn to God for our help, and as we grow in the Lord and understand the victory over sin that He has accomplished, we'll turn more and more quickly.

God's grace will bring us back into alignment with Him and His will. When we turn aside and experience symptoms of sin, we won't run *away* from the Lord, we'll run *to* Him. For example, when I feel irritation over petty things (which still happens far too often), I turn to the Lord and trust Him to be glad to be with me even in my messiness. I trust Him to return me to joy and peace.[3]

> *I have found that when I focus on my sin, whatever it is, it's a cycle of sin and guilt and failure, but when I focus on Jesus, my self slips away, and that's when I start finding freedom from the sin that had trapped me.*[4]

Take in this good news from the first part of Romans 8—read it as if you've never seen it before. There's a great contrast set up here between the flesh life (described in Romans 7) and the Spirit-to-spirit life. If you look to the Lord by faith, you can live in Romans 8, as Paul did. Here is Romans 8:1-4 and 9a.

> *There is therefore now no condemnation*
> *for those who are in Christ Jesus.*
> *For the law of the Spirit of life has set you free in Christ Jesus*
> *from the law of sin and death.*
> *For God has done what the law, weakened by the flesh, could not do:*
> *by sending his own Son in the likeness of sinful flesh and for sin,*
> *he condemned sin in the flesh,*
> *in order that the righteous requirement of the law*
> *might be fulfilled in us,*
> *who walk not according to the flesh but according to the Spirit. . . .*
> *You, however, are not in the flesh but in the Spirit,*
> *if in fact the Spirit of God dwells in you.*

---

[3] For more on this see, the work of Marcus Warner, Jim Wilder, Karl Lehman, and others, available at Deeper Walk International, deeperwalkinternational.org.

[4] Bethany Sowell, personal correspondence, June 27, 2022. Used by permission.

That is what God accomplished for you. It is worthy of significant meditation.

Sin in the life of those in the kingdom of darkness

Before I speak of sin in the life of the Christian living by self-effort, what of an unbeliever, even one who pretends to be a real Christian? Romans 8:7-9 describes this person.

> *The mind that is set on the flesh is hostile to God,*
> *for it does not submit to God's law; indeed, it cannot.*
> *Those who are in the flesh cannot please God....*
> *Anyone who does not have the Spirit of Christ*
> *does not belong to him.*

This hostile heart may look good on the outside, but it is not at all uncommon for this person to go into deeper and deeper places of destruction, into increasingly egregious sin, often while still appearing as a "servant of righteousness."[5]

Increasingly egregious sin indicates an increasing hardness of heart, or as 1 Timothy 4:1-2 says, a "seared conscience."

> *Now the Spirit expressly says that in later times*
> *some will depart from the faith*
> *by devoting themselves to deceitful spirits and teachings of demons,*
> *through the insincerity of liars whose consciences are seared.*[6]

Sin in the life of a Christian living by self-effort

Romans and other New Testament epistles refer to living the Christian life by self-effort as "living according to the flesh." In

---

[5] 2 Corinthians 11:12-15.

[6] See "Conscience in the Bible: Insight into Abusers and Their Targets," *Here's the Joy*, April 20, 2017, https://heresthejoy.com/2017/04/conscience-in-the-bible-insight-into-abusers-and-their-targets/ Also "the Defiled Conscience: Should We Lovingly Help or Sharply Rebuke?" *Here's the Joy*, May 16, 2017, https://heresthejoy.com/2017/05/the-defiled-conscience-should-we-lovingly-help-or-sharply-rebuke/

Romans 8:5-6 we see the contrast, phrase by phrase, between the flesh and the Spirit.

> *For those who live according to the flesh*
> *set their minds on the things of the flesh,*
> *but those who live according to the Spirit*
> *set their minds on the things of the Spirit.*
> *For to set the mind on the flesh is death,*
> *but to set the mind on the Spirit is life and peace.*

Romans 8 has much more to say about life in the Spirit. But right now it's important to look at that contrast. If a Christian is living by his own self-effort, he will live the floundering life of Romans 7, further described in Romans 8:5-6 above. I talk about that miserable cycle in the next chapter.

If for some reason she or he has a divided heart, then there will often be struggles she may not understand until she recognizes that dividedness and brings it to the Lord.[7]

But in general, the journey does not need to be a long struggle.

> *When I first started this Christian journey 5 years ago I used to twist and kick myself horribly each time I acted in a sinful way after understanding what sin was to God. I'd come crawling back to God upset that "I'd disappointed Him **again**"! I would think He must regret the day He adopted me into His family!*
>
> *Each time, He just waited patiently until I had stopped verbally beating up on myself on His behalf and gently let me know me it was okay, that He forgave me. It was okay because I would best grow with Him if I understood I was imperfect still in this world and needed **Him** to help me see; and in seeing my mistakes with His eyes, He could take that mistake and in His wisdom and guidance to walk closer with Him so I could use His presence to help*

---

[7] This would include the "dividedness" that comes not just from personal sin, but also from trauma experienced at the hands of others.

me do better each and every day, knowing there was no condemnation, just encouragement and love.

There is a saying that the person who makes no mistakes in learning a skill will never be as skilled or valuable as the person who made mistakes, recognized those mistakes, and learned to avoid making the same ones again. I think God wants us to learn that in our Christian walk also. I quit cowering at making a mistake or sin and began to trust that the Holy Spirit would help me make the best decisions, and if I did mess up, He would help me acknowledge and recognize it and look up to God for His wisdom in how to handle that situation better the next time. It has helped me so much and brought me closer to God daily! His strength in my weakness makes such a difference.[8]

This is what it means to be "free from sin." And this brings to mind a conversation I had with a friend.

Can we really be free from sin?

"How can I pray for you?" I asked my friend.

She mentioned a few things. Then she hesitated. "I have so much trouble with sin," she said. "I keep sinning. I feel suspicious of people, that they don't like me. I'm so jealous—I see other people doing well, and I feel full of jealousy. Just sin, all the time."

I could have chuckled and said, "Welcome to the club of humanity." But I didn't.

We prayed together for deliverance and victory. Then I asked, "Tell me, tell me how it all proceeds. When you sense the sin in you, what happens? What do you do?"

She said, "Well, first I don't want to admit it. At first I try to ignore it or make excuses for it, because I don't want to acknowledge that it's there.

---

[8] Linda Hart, personal correspondence, June 28, 2022. Used by permission.

"And then . . ." she continued, "then I finally admit it, and I say I'm sorry."

"And then what?" I asked.

"What do you mean?"

"What happens after that? After you say you're sorry? Do you do anything else? Does God say or do anything?"

"No. I just say I'm sorry, and that's all."

This is a hard place to be, especially for a Christian with a tender conscience, one who really wants to live a life well-pleasing to God. The problem is that there seems to be a veritable bottomless cesspool of sin that can keep bubbling up with its noxious fumes, invading the thoughts and even pervading the life.

"I'm sorry," we say. And "I'm so sorry," we say again. And on and on and on it goes.

And no wonder we don't want to acknowledge it when it appears, because it's one more evidence that we don't have victory, that our attempts are futile, that we're full, full, full of sin. When we stop to acknowledge it, it seems simply overwhelming. Discouraging and depressing, to the point of despair.

We struggle. We want to be thankful for forgiveness, but we feel stuck in a vicious cycle of sin-sorry-struggle-sin-sorry-struggle, when the Bible seems to indicate that there has got to be something more to the Christian life.

So I proposed a new plan of attack, one that I'm putting to work in my own life, not at all flawlessly, but in faith.

First, when you see the sin in you, don't ignore it or make excuses for it. Acknowledge it immediately.

But don't despair! First, thank God, that your sin never takes Him by surprise, and also, that He's kind enough to allow you to be aware of it. Because He is *a good God*, gracious and kind and loving, and your awareness indicates that you are not hardhearted.

Thank Him that because you are "free from sin," according to Romans 6:18, you can walk away. You can turn from it. This will sometimes include an "I'm sorry," but it would always include a sense of seeing the truth and the right way, in line with the real meaning of Biblical "repentance."

If I gaze only on my sin, it can start feeling like I'm watching disgusting, noxious fumes burble up from the depths of my soul. I can fall into deep despair and feel no sense of relief.

So that's not where I go. There's another step, and this is the step that eventually leads to more and more victory.

After acknowledging the sin and turning from it, *look to Jesus*.
First of all, to the Jesus who died on the cross
to pay for this sin and more,
but then to the Jesus who rose from the grave.
Not just victorious over death, but victorious *over sin*.

This is important for you personally, because Colossians 3 says that if you're a real Christian, *you've risen with Him*.

Have you died to sin? If you've trusted in Jesus Christ for your salvation, the Scriptures say you have. Read Romans 6:2-18 (NET) here, as if you're seeing it for the first time:

> *How can we who died to sin still live in it?*
> *Or do you not know*
> *that as many as were baptized into Christ Jesus*
> *were baptized into his death?*
> *Therefore we have been buried with him through baptism*
> *into death,*
> *in order that just as Christ was raised from the dead*
> *through the glory of the Father,*
> *so we too may live a new life.*
> *For if we have become united with him in the likeness of his death,*
> *we will certainly also be united in the likeness of his resurrection.*
> *We know that our old man was crucified with him*
> ***so that the body of sin would no longer dominate us,***

so that we would no longer be enslaved to sin.
(For someone who has died has been freed from sin.)
Now if we died with Christ,
we believe that we will also live with him.
We know that since Christ has been raised from the dead,
he is never going to die again; death no longer has mastery over him.
For the death he died, he died to sin once for all, but the life he lives,
he lives to God.
So you too consider yourselves dead to sin,
but alive to God in Christ Jesus.
Therefore do not let sin reign in your mortal body
so that you obey its desires,
and do not present your members to sin
as instruments to be used for unrighteousness,
but present yourselves to God as those who are alive from the
dead and your members to God
as instruments to be used for righteousness.
For sin will have no mastery over you,
because you are not under law but under grace.
What then?
Shall we sin because we are not under law but under grace?
Absolutely not!
Do you not know that if you present yourselves as obedient slaves,
you are slaves of the one you obey,
either of sin resulting in death,
or obedience resulting in righteousness?
But thanks be to God that though you were slaves to sin,
you obeyed from the heart that pattern of teaching
you were entrusted to,
and having been freed from sin,
you became enslaved to righteousness.

What does this mean? Ask the Holy Spirit to open your eyes. Grapple with it. Like Jacob with the angel,[9] don't let Him go until He blesses you with understanding of that truth.

Yes, look at your sin. In some cases, you may need to weep over it.

But even more, gaze at your Savior. It is through our focusing on Him in faith that our lives will be transformed.

You can go beyond simply being thankful that once again you're forgiven, though there is much to be thankful for in that. You can go beyond that, to expecting,[10] anticipating, that either little by little or all at once, your besetting sins will fall away and will no longer have that grip on you that they now seem to have. And because of the power of Jesus Christ, this victory doesn't have to wait for the next life, but can happen on this earth.

**You can drink long and deep of His living water,
to know Him and His full salvation, yes, even here in this life,
in the realm of the spirit.
We can joyfully anticipate much victory over sin
and delight in the things of God,
through the resurrection power of the Living Savior.**

I'm not talking about being sinless or flawless, but about being, in the power of the Holy Spirit, what Jesus Christ Himself promised us we could be.[11] Free from sin. You are not enslaved to it. By His power, you can walk free.

"You've given me a lot to think about," said my friend.

So with her permission I'm writing it here, as a reminder for her, and for me.

---

[9] Genesis 32:26.

[10] See "What Can We Expect from God?" *Here's the Joy*, July 20, 2022. https://heresthejoy.com/2022/07/what-can-we-expect-from-god/

[11] "Somebody's Perfect?" *Here's the Joy*, April 29, 2012, https://heresthejoy.com/2012/04/somebodys-perfect/

UNTWISTED TRUTH FROM CHAPTER 15

❖ The Bible crucially distinguishes among (1) the Christian who loves God and walks by faith in the power of the Holy Spirit, (2) the Christian who loves God but is trying to live the Christian life by his own self-effort, (3) the lost person who is outside the Kingdom of God, and (4) the wicked who are set against God. When we read Scripture, especially the New Testament, it is important to understand these distinctions.

❖ Romans tells us that we are free from sin. (Not "will be" but "are.") This means we are not bound to it and can walk away from it.

❖ The way to experience this freedom is to continue to look to Jesus in faith.

CHAPTER 16

"Look To the Cross More": A Response to the "Gospel-Centered" Movement

A while back I received a letter from a friend. She said:

> *In the Reformed/Gospel-centered movement, the focus seems to be on how sinful and wicked and powerless we all are and how comforted and relieved we should be when we look to the cross. It seems like the answer to most problems is to look to the cross more. I don't even know exactly what that means. For me, it encouraged a miserable cycle of wallowing in how awful I am and basing the Christian life on the feelings I get when I think of Jesus dying for me.*[1]

Here is my reply.

Dear friend,
Thank you for this—you've put into words something that has concerned me for years. I've written about various aspects of it,

---

[1] "Look to the Cross More: A Response to the Gospel-Centered Movement," *Here's the Joy*, September 16, 2019. https://heresthejoy.com/2019/09/look-to-the-cross-more-a-response-to-the-gospel-centered-movement/

but your letter pulls several of those concepts together. You'll notice parts of your paragraph reflected in my headings.

The "Gospel-centered" movement, our sinfulness, and "looking to the cross"

I came into the "Reformed/Gospel-centered movement" in 2007, unaware of anything regarding any sort of movement. I remember listening to my first C.J. Mahaney sermon that same year, from a CD a friend lent me, in which Mahaney said that [whatever it was he was telling us to do] was *because of the gospel.*

I appreciated this, because I loved thinking about all of life being for the sake of the gospel, which has a non-elusive definition to me, as being the good news of the life, death, resurrection, ascension, and seating of our Lord Jesus Christ, for the salvation of souls and the transformation of lives. It didn't cross my mind that others who taught using the term might be using it differently.

As time went on, I heard "the gospel" used more and more with what seemed to me like less and less clarity. I began to wonder what people meant when they talked about it. I wrote about it in 2010,[2] observing how for some reason "the gospel" in many cases seemed to be replacing Jesus Christ Himself.

Yes, I also observed how much emphasis Mahaney and some others put on the utter vile wretched sinfulness of . . . those who have been redeemed by the Spirit of God.

I also observed that the focus seemed to be overbalanced on "the cross." Hardly ever the Resurrection, which was supremely puzzling to me. And certainly not the Ascension and Seating. (Who in evangelicalism talks about those, unless you happen to be studying through Ephesians or Hebrews? And usually the barest mention even then.)

---

[2] "Should My Life Be Centered Around the Gospel?" *Here's the Joy,* August 28, 2010. https://heresthejoy.com/2010/08/should-my-life-be-centered-around-the-gospel

And I noticed again that sometimes these speakers and leaders would talk about "the cross" when they should have been talking about Jesus Christ Himself.

Glorying in the cross according to Galatians 6:14

In my puzzlement trying to understand why the focus on "the cross," I figured people had taken Galatians 6:14 out of balance. Here it is in the KJV:

> *But God forbid that I should glory,*
> *save in the cross of our Lord Jesus Christ,*
> *by whom the world is crucified unto me,*
> *and I unto the world.*

But both common sense and a study of the Scriptures would show that this doesn't mean we should preach the cross only and glory in nothing else. Paul himself, for example, gloried in the souls who were coming to Christ through his ministry (Romans 15:17, 1 Thessalonians 2:20).

Paul wrote this Galatians passage with this extreme wording about the cross because the preaching of the cross—the most ignominious device for public execution—was a reproach, a point of mocking, making Christians and Christianity a laughingstock. Paul vigorously pushed back with, "Nay! His death on the cross is how Jesus Christ secured forgiveness of sins for those who trust in Him! I'll not only preach it, I will glory in preaching it!"

But it has seemed in recent years that some Christians haven't understood the context, and as a result they have focused on "the cross" to the exclusion of other extremely important truths.

Basing the Christian life on the feelings I get (comfort and relief) when I think of Jesus dying for me

Over the past decade and more I've observed what your letter describes. Surely not in all churches in this movement, but it seems to be true of many. That is, urging Christians to focus on our own sinfulness, as Mahaney said, "Staying close to the doctrine of sin."[3] Urging us to "look to the cross more," to try to meditate more on the fact that we're forgiven.

The "comfort and relief" you mention in your letter are to be based on the gratefulness you're supposed to be flooded with as you meditate on "the cross." (This will mean that when anyone asks you how you're doing, you'll say, "better than I deserve," because you deserve hell.)[4] And then that gratitude is supposed to motivate you to good works.

Now of course, gratitude is a wonderful and important thing. And God gave us an absolutely incredible gift by giving us His Son, for which we are supremely grateful. This is why it took several years before I could put words to what bothered me about this focus on gratitude. The result was an article about how Gratitude Motivation is not sufficient for living the Christian life—and what is.[5]

The "miserable cycle"

Your letter mentions feelings of comfort and relief that you're supposed to have when you "look to the cross more." But this teaching is actually designed to produce a Christian life that is of a cyclical nature, so those feelings of comfort and relief are supposed to be relatively short-lived. You are supposed to go back to feeling yourself to be a wretched sinner, and if you don't, then by the same teaching, that means you're arrogant and self-righteous.

So this is how the cycle is supposed to proceed:

1. You, as a blood-bought and redeemed child of God, meditate on what a wretched, vile sinner you are.

2. For relief from your horror at your own inexhaustible well of sin, you meditate on "the cross."

---

[3] See p 54.

[4] *Untwisting Scriptures that were used to tie you up, gag you, and tangle your mind: Book 3 Your Words, Your Emotions,* Pennycress Publishing 2021, pp 99-102.

[5] "A Better Motivation for Christian Service than Gratitude," *Here's the Joy,* December 19, 2017, https://heresthejoy.com/2017/12/even-christmas-gratitude-isnt-my-motivator-to-serve-god/

3. As you meditate on that, you are filled with gratitude that Jesus would suffer that terrible death for such a depraved and wretched and worthless sinner as yourself.

4. This gratitude then motivates you to good works, which are often defined by your church rather than your having space to listen to the Holy Spirit yourself.

BUT in spite of your good works the cycle continues, because:

5. The good works are done in the strength of the flesh. I know this, because the formula above doesn't include spiritual transformation and walking in the Holy Spirit and listening to His voice and acknowledging the spiritual battle coming from the enemy's fiery darts. Because of this (and perhaps some other reasons), these good works will feel like *never enough*.

6. You get exhausted, because working for the Lord out of your own strength is always exhausting and can feel like He's a harsh taskmaster. The work feels futile or unsatisfying or too difficult.

7. You wonder "is this really all there is?" and then you feel guilty for being dissatisfied in the work you're doing. Sometimes you might want to receive some sort of earthly reward for your work. Maybe you take your frustrations out on someone else, causing them pain.

8. Then you feel even more guilty.

9. You see that your emotions are "all over the place," so instead of ever being told to listen to your emotions to find out what's going on inside, you're told that you're supposed to train your emotions to be "godly emotions."[6] (The truth is that your emotions are telling you something important you need to know about yourself. Whether they're based on truth or lies, they need to be heard and understood.)[7]

---

[6] Nicole Whitacre, "How Not To Be The Charlie Browniest," *Girl Talk,* December 11, 2017, http://girltalkhome.com/blog/how-not-to-be-the-charlie-browniest/

[7] "Does Reason Really Trump Emotion?" *Untwisting Scriptures that were used to tie you up, gag you, and tangle your mind: Book 3 Your Words, Your Emotions,* Pennycress Publishing 2021, pp 109-120.

10. You bemoan the wretched sinfulness of your heart, which appears to be affirming the truth of what the preacher preached.

11. The cycle begins again.

And this is only a very mild presentation of the most mild version of the problem. I didn't even factor in what it looks like when abusers are in charge of the cycle. At every stage they will be glad to (either harshly or gently) affirm what a vile wretch you are. They will (either gently or harshly) point out your ungratefulness and dissatisfaction and failure to measure up.

They will be more than glad to ordain what your "good works" should look like, and often that will mean building their own kingdom, the kingdom of man, disguised to look like the Kingdom of God. I've heard celebrity preachers vilely mock church members for thinking they can be led by the Spirit for ministry outside of "serving the church" as the leaders decree.[8]

> *It has always stumped me how we can follow Jesus' admonition to abide in Him and bring forth fruit while also checking all the church-decreed activities off a weekly list that we must explicitly follow to be considered in good standing.*[9]

They will do all this with varying degrees of finesse, depending on how skilled they are at their role of Wolf in Sheep's Clothing.

I also didn't factor in the possibility that the teachings that promote this cycle can be aimed at victims and survivors of all kinds of abuse and trauma. For them, the reactions to the various parts of this cycle can be far more extreme.

It is truly a miserable cycle. . . .

But there is a better way.

---

[8] For one example, see "The Vision of James MacDonald, Mega-Church Pastor Who Sues Bloggers' Wives," *Here's the Joy,* November 19, 2018, https://heresthejoy.com/2018/11/the-vision-of-james-macdonald-mega-church-pastor-who-sues-bloggers-wives/

[9] Tina Wood, personal correspondence, June 22, 2022.

CHAPTER 16 – A RESPONSE TO "LOOK TO THE CROSS MORE"

The better way

The better way is the reason I originally began writing on my website back in 2009. Some of the understandings I'm describing in this chapter came years after I started writing at *Here's the Joy,* but my primary purpose then was to talk about the "other part" of the gospel—not just the change of destination, but the change of our entire lives, right here on earth, because of what Jesus accomplished for us. Like . . .

➢ The change from doing your work in the strength of the flesh to doing it in the power of the Spirit.

➢ The change to understanding that Christians are engaged in a spiritual battle with genuinely real spiritual entities of evil that need to be understood.[10]

➢ The change to being unafraid of your emotions, knowing that they are giving you an indication of what's going on inside you, to be able to face them without shame, which can better help you understand yourself and your past.[11]

➢ The change to understanding that in Jesus Christ you have indeed been set free from sin.

➢ The change to knowing that you are actually His beloved sheep, and yes, you can actually hear His voice in your spirit and respond to Him.

➢ The change from despair to joy in living the Christian life.

This is the better way, the way we can flourish in our Christian lives. In the deep places of your spirit, you can focus on how powerful and good our Lord Jesus Christ is. You can focus on how He has accomplished all your salvation, both in eternity and right now, having provided all you need to live and walk in victory now.

---

[10] For more on this, see *Prayer Armor for Defense Against the Enemy's Flaming Darts*, Pennycress Publishing, 2019.

[11] More on this in *Untwisting Scriptures that were used to tie you up, gag you, and tangle your mind: Book 3, Your Words, Your Emotions*, Pennycress Publishing, 2021.

The answer to many spiritual problems will be to look to Him, understanding that He has given you His Holy Spirit to commune with your own spirit about truth regarding who He is and who you are, so that truth will take root in the deepest places of your soul.

Look to Him, understanding that He has equipped you to fight the inevitable spiritual battles. These spiritual battles will be waged not just against your own sin (which He gladly frees you from), but also—and I might even say primarily—against the evil in the world around you that is destroying lost souls.

When you read the Scriptures, this "gospel" can be the overarching template into which everything fits. You can expect that the living water Jesus promised in John 7 will flow in and through you to others, in whatever way He leads.

> Knowing you can live the Christian life free of fear, guilt, or shame,
>
> knowing God loves you and delights to be with you,
>
> asking God to continue to show you whatever needs to change about your life and to accomplish those changes in you,
>
> being willing to learn from your varied emotions,
>
> loving Him without fear that every turning aside will cut Him off from you,
>
> recognizing that you don't need to be stuck in the crazy cycle of sin-sorry-struggle-sin-sorry-struggle,
>
> and trusting Him to lead you step by step by His Holy Spirit,

. . . you can be confident that He is empowering you to accomplish whatever good work He may call you to, because He is powerful, He is good, and He loves you.

And yes, this truly is "good news." Almost too good to be true. Almost.

Love,
Rebecca

CHAPTER 16 – A RESPONSE TO "LOOK TO THE CROSS MORE"

UNTWISTED TRUTH FROM CHAPTER 16

❖ "Glorying in the cross," for Paul, meant he was not ashamed of the cross of Jesus Christ, not that the cross should be our only focus in our Christian lives.

❖ Gratitude for Jesus' death for me is not sufficient motivation for good works in the Christian life.

❖ The "miserable cycle" of meditating on your vileness as a sinner, being grateful for the cross, and then being motivated to good works, will fail every time because it is done in the strength of the flesh.

❖ This cycle will continue downward, apparently confirming that you are nothing but a wretched sinner constantly in need of forgiveness.

❖ The transformation that our Lord Jesus Christ offers in "the rest of the gospel" can ultimately affect you in every area of your life.

Scripture Index

Genesis
32:26   p 163 footnote

2 Samuel
2   p 92
12   p 93

Psalms
1:6   p 92
5:12   p 92
7   p 94
26:1   p 92
27   p 94
31   p 94
34   p 94
37   p 94
109   p 94

Proverbs
4:18   p 20
17:15   p 42

Isaiah
9:2   p 143 footnote
53   p 25
53:6   p 23
61:10   p 14

Jeremiah
17:9   p 13 footnote

Ezekiel
22   p 109
34   pp 85, 109
34:2   p 112

Matthew
3:2   p 142
4:16   p 143 footnote
6:2,5,16   p 81
6:33   p 59
6:33   p 69 footnote
7   p 91
7:3-5   pp 81, 89, 95
7:4-5   pp 91, 92 footnote
7:15   p 108
7:15-17   p 124
9:36   p 28
10   p 107
10:16   pp 25, 125
15:7-9   p 82
16:6   p 82
17:15-2   p 108
18:10   p 85 footnote
20:27   p 59
22:36-40   p 38 footnote
22:37-38   p 59
23:13, 15   p 85
23:13-33   p 136
23:14,25-28   pp 84
23:23   pp 38 footnote, 83
23:29-32   p 135

Mark
14:65   p 133

Luke
3:8   p 124
10   p 107
10:2   p 116
12:32   p 26
12:47-48   p 41
15   pp 17, 26
15:22   p 59
16:10   p 39
19:47   p 59
22:53   p 135
22:63-65   p 133

John
5:44	p 69 footnote
7	p 174
7:24	p 123
7:37-39	p 27
8:7	p 40
10	pp 25, 26
10:12-13	p 116
16:20-22	p 144
19	p 42 footnote
19:11	p 41

Acts
2	pp 42, 92
2:14-40	p 42
13:50	p 59
17	p 92
20:27-32	p 111
26:18	p 145
26:20	p 145

Romans
1	pp 46, 49
1:18-32	p 47
2	pp 45, 49, 51
2:17	p 48
2:17-24	p 50
3:1-2	p 59
5:6	p 36 footnote
5:17	p 12
6:2-18	p 162
6:17-18	p 155
6:18	pp 156, 161
7	pp 20, 63 footnote, 157, 159
8:1	p 65
8:1-4, 9a	p 157
8:5-6	p 159
8:7-9	p 158
8:17	p 13, 27
8:37	p 12
15:17	p 169
17-24	p 49

1 Corinthians
1:30	p 27
6:11	p 13
6:17	p 13
6:19	p 27
10:24	p 69 footnote
11:1	p 61
12:27	pp 12, 27

2 Corinthians
1:21-22	p 12
2:12-14	p 64
4:1-2	p 63
4:6	p 153
4:7	p 27
5:17-21	p 12
7:9	p 149
10:5	p 64
11:3	p 112
11:12-15	p 158 footnote
11:13-15	p 122

Galatians
2:11-21	p 42 footnote
3:29	p 27
5:16-17	p 46
5:19-21	p 125
5:22-25	pp 124, 130
6:14	p 169

Ephesians
1:1	p 12
2:6	p 12
2:18	p 12
5:6-17	p 123
6	p 28
6:10-18	p 27

Colossians
1:13	p 155 footnote
2:10	p 12
3	p 162
3:1-2	p 69 footnote
3:1-4	p 144 footnote
3:12	p 12

SCRIPTURE INDEX

1 Thessalonians
2:20   p 169

1 Timothy
1:12   p 37
1:13   p 50 footnote
1:15   pp 59, 60
1:15-16   pp 57, 58, 65
1:16   p 60
3:1-7   p 125
3:2-3   p 113 footnote
4:1-2   p 158 footnote

2 Timothy
3:12-13   p 122

Titus
1:6-8   p 113 footnote
1:6-9   p 125

Hebrews
11   p 122
11:6   p 69 footnote

James
2:10   p 38
3   p 27

1 Peter
2:5   p 27
2:9   p 13
2:25   p 26
5:1-5   p 116
5:2-3   p 26

2 Peter
1:3-4   p 12

1 John
4:1   p 123

Jude
4   p 126

179

About the Author

Since 2006 Rebecca Davis has been studying and learning about abuse and trauma, especially through the first-person accounts of many of her friends. For about thirty years longer than that, she has been an avid student of the Scriptures.

Rebecca has enjoyed teaching truth to many through the years about topics as diverse as the realities of abuse, hope through the grief of Alzheimer's, miracles and gospel opportunities in the lives of missionaries, the true freedom and gracious life transformation to be found in Jesus Christ, and, of course, untwisting Scriptures.

She is the author or collaborating author of over 20 books for children and adults. Her adult books are written to help Christians have a deeper understanding of the true God and His love for them, to help those who have been abused find hope in the Lord Jesus Christ, and to help Christians better understand how they can help those in need. This is her desire for this book, the fourth in the *Untwisting Scriptures* series.

Rebecca enjoys meeting with friends, listening to their stories, and offering hope through Jesus Christ. She and her husband Tim have four children and three grandchildren. You can connect with her at her blog, heresthejoy.com. You can also see Rebecca's work as a trauma-informed book coach and ghostwriter at rebeccadaviswordworking.com.

Made in the USA
Monee, IL
02 January 2023